H. G. Ganss

History of St. Patrick's Church, Carlisle, Pennsylvania

H. G. Ganss

History of St. Patrick's Church, Carlisle, Pennsylvania

ISBN/EAN: 9783743326804

Manufactured in Europe, USA, Canada, Australia, Japa

Cover: Foto ©ninafisch / pixelio.de

Manufactured and distributed by brebook publishing software (www.brebook.com)

H. G. Ganss

History of St. Patrick's Church, Carlisle, Pennsylvania

HISTORY

—OF—

St. Patrick's Church,

CARLISLE, PENNSYLVANIA.

—BY—

REV. H. G. GANSS, DOC. MUS.

PHILADELPHIA:
D. J. GALLAGHER & CO.
1895.

HISTORY OF ST. PATRICK'S CHURCH,

CARLISLE, PENNSYLVANIA.

BY REV. H. G. GANSS.

INTRODUCTION.

The divine commission, "*Go teach all nations*," has been one to which the Catholic Church has ever been true and faithful : one woven like a tissue of gold in her nineteen-centuried history ; one inseparably connected with the divinity of her organization and existence. After the pentecostal outpouring of the Holy Spirit, she entered upon her stupendous mission with marks and prerogatives in which the whole human family from the uncultured Lombard and Goth to the erudite Greek and Roman, discerned the presence of gifts which belong to the supernatural order and of graces which connect her by an almost visible bond with the unseen world. These gifts and graces, as history records, have been her inheritance, not only in apostolic ages, but are poured out as lavishly in our own generation as in any that preceded it. It is by this token, and not by numerical success, that we recognize the apostolic commission.

St. Paul's mission was the same when pursued and stoned by the mob at Lystra, as when his disciples embraced and kissed him "*sorrowing that they should see his face no more.*"

The Church never changes, is the complaint of her adversaries. They might with the same truthfulness say that her apostles and missionaries likewise never change, from St. Stephen and St. Paul to the sainted successors whose careers may be touched upon in these pages.

The missionary spirit is the outgrowth of Christianity; the missionary the lineal descendant of the apostle. In reading profane history we never encounter that yearning desire, unswerving zeal, tireless energy, not to mention the spirit of total self-abandonment and absorption of every personal motive, to bring men to a higher sphere of morality or spirituality. To save one soul the missionary cheerfully makes the sacrifice. The ancient philosophers, no matter how enthusiastic in the advocacy of their doctrines, never left the pleasant haunts of Academus or the alluring pleasures of Athens, under the guidance of a humane, sublime impulse to instruct the ignorant, console the sorrowing, ameliorate the wretchedness of the oppressed, lift up the downtrodden, or sow the seeds of peace and tranquility among hostile nations.

This has been the divinely appointed mission of the Church—a mission in which she has been always faithful, nor has ever faltered. Her ambassadors paled before no obstacle, shrank from no danger, were disheartened by no failure.—" Neither oceans nor tempests, neither the ices of the pole nor the heat of the tropics can damp their zeal," says Chateaubriand. They live with the Esquimaux in his seal-skin cabin: they subsist on train-oil with the Greenlander: they traverse the solitude with the Tartar or the Iroquois: they mount the dromedary of the Arab or accompany the wandering Caffir in his burning deserts, * * * * Not an island, not a rock in the ocean, has escaped their zeal; and as of old, the kingdoms of the earth were inadequate to the ambition of Alexander, so the globe is too contracted for their charity."*

With the first settlement of this newly discovered country, actuated by the dream of wealth or the excitement of adventure, in search of social advancement or in pursuit of political ambition, fleeing from religious persecution or fugitives from political tyranny, naturally a heterogeneous element crowded our shores.† Cut from the secure moorings of godly homes, untouched by religious influences, unhampered by legal restraints, amidst environments calculated to sound the manhood and search the faith of the strongest—many souls were swerv-

---

* Chateaubriand—*Genius of Christianity*, Book IV, p. 557.

† "Tyranny and injustice peopled America with men nurtured in suffering and adversity. The history of our colonization is the history of the crimes of Europe."—Bancroft, VII, 14. (Throughout this Paper the Boston (1879) edition of Bancroft's Work) has been used.

ing in their loyalty, wandering in a state of religious despondency, infected with the incipient stages of indifferentism, that would finally culminate in unbelief and apostasy. Nor is this to be wondered at, taking in view the well-nigh insurmountable obstacles that awaited the "papist," the barriers both legal and social that handicapped his material prosperity, and the blandishments and inducements held out by worldly considerations that tried his soul.

To the ministers of the true Faith, this sight aroused anxiety and caused alarm. They turned their eyes to the distant shores, saw the soul in peril on account of the lack of spiritual sustenance, saw many unable to cope with the temptations held out on the verge of apostasy, saw others with their dying lips pray for the sweet consolations of Holy Church which came not. The missionary spirit at once grasped the situation; its agents were true to their holy vocations and apostolic traditions. They came fired with burning zeal. Though they had to encounter cruel and superstitious peoples; had to enter into the midst of barbarism and savagery; had to run counter to the prejudices of jealous nationality and fierce bigotry; though they had to penetrate trackless forests, wade through mephitic swamps, cross foaming torrents, ford treacherous rivers, climb inaccessible mountains, face griping hunger and parching thirst,—benumbing cold and exhausting heat,— they came full of sweetness and charity. In face of all, we find them ever dauntless, hopeful, patient and persevering,—with the crucifix in their hands, and the image of the Crucified in their hearts.

In the annals of early American history, surely the missionary will be awarded a high niche. His conquests though unseen were none the less factors in the development, peace and prosperity of the country. Or is not he whose life is spent in the recesses of the forest, who performs works of the loftiest heroism without applause, dies a painful death without a spectator, is consigned to his grave without a tear, and lies buried without an epitaph, his name even not in the ken of mankind,—all to procure eternal happiness to some unknown savage,—does not such a one point out to us the loftiest type of humanity which we are able to conceive?

"The salvation of one soul is worth more than the conquest of an empire," says the heroic Champlain. It was the keynote of missionary toil, prayers and martyrdom, and though undertaken by foreign priests having frequently but a most imperfect idea of the language and customs of the people whose hardships they shared, and from a human standpoint of calculation, totally unfitted for the work before them, in the Providence of God they brought about the most brilliant achievements, and laid the foundation deep and strong, of that spiritual edifice which now challenges the admiration of the nation. Alone and unaided they had to scale an almost immovable breastwork of opposition under a galling fire of invective, calumny and persecution. How they fulfilled their mission, how they accomplished their task, and the abiding and permanent result of some of their labors, can be gleaned from the few fragmentary and discursive pages that follow.

CHAPTER I.

STATUS OF CATHOLICS IN COLONIAL TIMES.—DISABILITIES OF EARLY CATHOLIC SETTLERS.

One of the most perplexing problems that confronts the cursory reader of Catholic history in colonial times, is the doubt, uncertainty and mystery that shrouds the original settlers of its creed in this country. The scant data that have been preserved and rescued, at times make the perplexity all the more impenetrable, and when the meagre traditions are stripped of the glamor of romance and the accretions of years, they are found at times lamentably defective in historic truthfulness, and afford but the faintest clue to historical research.

In a measure this may be accounted for by the anomalous position our co-religionists occupied. Their numerical smallness; the studied secretiveness that frequently surrounded their movements, was more a matter of necessity than choice. Again it may be explained by the poverty and helplessness on the one hand, and the covert antagonism, if not open hostility, on the other, that dogged their every footstep. An intolerant bigotry that amounted to virtual ostracism kept them from the more populous towns; penal laws that in effect made them disfranchised aliens, prevented their acquisition of property or barred the way to civic or military preferment; an ineradicable prejudice coupled their name with disloyalty. They are denounced as the creatures of a foreign potentate: decried as abettors of the French; branded as the ever helpful allies of the marauding and massacring Indian; watched as fomentors of discord, sworn foes of the State.

The birth of religious toleration was typically and specifically the outgrowth of American ideas, and forms one of the proud achievements of our national character, as well as an absorbing chapter in our history. The universal toleration, both civil and religious, which was heralded to the four quarters of the globe, and which Lord Brougham declared to be "the noblest innovation of modern times," though the exclusive product of American ideas, had all the same when closely studied, nothing more than a mere factitious existence. In inculcating this heaven-born principle, expediency did not always go hand in hand with justice, nor was the law meted out with any pretence to equity. Popery and treason were still universally accepted as convertible terms. Theorists and philosophers in the eighteenth century descanted garrulously and metaphysically on religious liberty, and in lurid colors portrayed the evils of intolerance and persecution for conscience' sake, but no approach towards such a consummation was ever seriously attempted. However, it was reserved for the framers of our National Constitution to formulate and promulgate the fundamental principle of government, that "every man should be at liberty to worship God according to the dictates of his individual conscience," and that a perpetual divorce between the national government and every form of religious establishment should be enforced. America was the first nation to enunciate the two laws of civil and religious liberty, the two greatest contributors to modern civilization, the two most important factors in the growth and prosperity of the nation, the evangel that made it the home of the oppressed, the asylum of the persecuted, the Utopia of poet and philosopher. Sad, however, is the reflection that in spite of vehement protests and diplomatic advocacy, it required nearly two centuries to vitalize these humane laws and make them embrace in their scope and comprehensiveness those for whose amelioration and protection they were first enacted. Nominally, religious liberty was permitted in a few colonies, but summarily denied in the majority of them. In all of them, however, the Catholic was specifically excluded from the rights and immunities of full citizenship, in so far that he could not hold a civil or military office without committing perjury or apostasy. With some qualifications the humane intentions of beneficent lawgivers were thwarted and made nugatory, not only by local enactments, but by an ineradicable bigotry, which even legal claims could not override. What William Penn, the most august and imposing figure of colonial times, could not succeed in bringing to the minds and hearts of the American people, a less devout man but more adroit statesman, Thomas Jefferson, finally engrafted on the constitution of the country. Could the former have brought his conceptions of universal toleration, civil and religious, to a successful termination, which, handicapped as he was by local obstacles and hereditary prejudices, seemed almost impossible, he would literally deserve the title of "emancipator," which now an admiring and grateful posterity can only acclaim him figuratively.

The evolution of religious toleration, from the vague promises held out by pioneers in this country, to its full and radiant accomplishment after nearly two centuries of strife and opposition, is a story particularly interesting to the Catholic. From the settlement of Virginia, in 1609, down to the period of the American Revolution, a man's full enjoyment or complete abridgement of his civil rights was entirely dependent on his ready conformity to the established religion dominant in the Province in which he lived. The humane enactments of a Lord Baltimore, a Roger Williams and a William Penn, on which the most fulsome praise is lavished, and which even then made the heart of humanity throb in admiration and pride, left no trace or vestige on colonial legislation. During the entire colonial period the Catholic was almost as much an alien, disfranchised and scorned, in this boasted land of liberty, as he was in his native country, from which he fled with a view of escaping the iron hand of persecution and eluding the espionage which would tear him from his altar and wean his children from the faith of their sainted ancestors. As long as he remained in a state of unobserved quiescence no attention and opposition was encountered, but as soon as he wished to verify the vaunting boast that liberty was after all no empty phrase, he was confronted by a clamor of protest and resentment that taught him the prudential lesson that flight was at times the better part of valor.

During the entire colonial period "we were essentially a nation of Protestants * * * * * and took similar (European) methods of maintaining and perpetuating our Protestantism, excluding those who dissented from it from sharing in the government and frankly adopting the policy which had prevailed in England from the time of Queen Elizabeth."* In other words the obnoxious and inhuman penal laws were transplanted to this new country and enforced with a pitiless severity, as far as civil preferment was concerned, only equalled by that of the countries from which the refugees had fled in quest of peace and liberty.

---

* Stillé—*Religious Tests in Provincial Pennsylvania*, p. 10.

In Virginia, where the English Church was established by law and sumptuously endowed, all men were obliged under severe penalties, vigorously enforced, to have their children baptized. Quakers and Catholics were expelled, and upon returning the third time were liable to capital punishment. In New England no quarter or mercy was ever shown to the Catholic. In 1691, a law was enacted in Massachusetts abrogating the barbarous brutalities perpetrated under the old theocracy,—permitting all Christians the exercise of their various beliefs—excepting, of course, Roman Catholics. However, only a Congregationalist could be a freeman, whilst all, irrespective of church affiliation, had to pay a tax to support the ministry of that particular denomination. In Maine, New Hampshire, and Connecticut the same system of intolerance was religiously in vogue, and conformity to the dominant sect was the pledge of civil liberty and the stepping stone to official life and business emoluments. In New York, Catholic priests were not permitted to set foot, and if discovered were escorted to the state boundary, and only surreptitiously, at the peril of their lives, could they baptize or administer the consolations of holy religion. The Catholic, though denied the exercise of his faith, was all the same compelled to pay an annual tax toward the support of Episcopal rectors, who had charge of the legally constituted parishes,—a charge having a mere geographical existence at times. In New Jersey, when the colony was under royal authority, in 1702, with much parade and display, liberty of conscience was trumpeted throughout the land to attract emigrants. Papists and Quakers were again specifically excluded. In Maryland* the English Church was established in 1696, and its first official act was to disfranchise the very Catholics and their children who were the first to proclaim religion on these shores in 1649. In Carolina an act was passed in 1704, requiring all members of the Assembly to partake of the sacrament of the Lord's Supper according to the rites of the Church of England. Georgia following the precedents established, gave religious freedom to all sects and denominations—but withheld it from the " Papists."

Thus we see in all the colonies, he who did not conform to the established religion of the colony in which he lived, whether it was Episcopalianism or Congregationalism, had his liberties not only curtailed, and his way

---

* " The Catholic Proprietaries in Maryland were the first to grant religious toleration (1666) and emigrants arrived from every clime ; and the colonial legislature extended its sympathies to many nations as well as sects. From France came Huguenots, from Germany, from Holland, from Sweden, from Finnland, I believe from Piedmont the children of misfortune sought protection under the tolerant sceptre of the Roman Catholic,"*—and fifteen years later (1681),—" Roman Catholics were disfranchised in the province they had planted."† " On the soil which long before Locke pleaded for toleration or Penn for religious freedom, a Catholic proprietary had opened to Protestants, the Catholic inhabitants became the victim of Anglican intolerance, Mass might not be said publicly. No Catholic might teach the young. If the wayward child of a papist would but become an apostate, the law wrested from his parents a share of their property. * * * * * Such were the methods adopted to prevent the growth of popery."‡

* Bancroft, vol. II, p. 4. † *Ibid.*, p. 8. ‡ *Ibid.*, p. 212.

barred to civil office or military promotion, but was at the same time compelled to support by irksome taxation the arbitrary despotism that oppressed him, which was all the more galling, cloaked as it was in the garb of religion. As for the Catholic, like the negro in slavery days, he had no constitutional rights that need be respected. He was disfranchised and allowed to eke out an existence more from motives of pity than love of justice. He could neither vote nor hold office, was compelled to support a creed and ministry, both of which he held in abhorrence and detestation. He was the sport and victim of the most contracted bigotry, which at times assumed the attitude of bitter hostility and cruel persecution.

But was there not a more tolerant and friendly spirit manifested in Pennsylvania towards the Catholic and dissenter? Was not the land of Penn during the provincial period heralded throughout the civilized world as the classic land of religious liberty, where liberty of conscience was the corner-stone of the foundation upon which the commonwealth was erected? Was it a vain boast or rhetorical bombast when Edmund Burke said "All persons who profess to believe in one God are freely tolerated, and those who believe in Jesus Christ, of whatsoever denomination, are not excluded from employment and posts?"

It is true that in Pennsylvania an ameliorated and more just condition of affairs presents itself. Dissenters and

"Papists" were not burned because they were heretics, nor banished because they were schismatics. It is again true, there was no established Church to be supported by legal taxation, and the public exercise of religion met with a charitable connivance if not tacit toleration. At this period the modest St. Joseph's Chapel, in Willing's Alley, Philadelphia, was used for Catholic services, and there can be no doubt that "it was the only place in the original thirteen States where Mass was permitted to be publicly celebrated prior to the Revolution." Yet this reluctant toleration was permitted more in the nature of a favor than granted as an inalienable right. All prospects of the Catholic sharing in the full rights and privileges of citizenship were set at naught by one insuperable barrier—the obnoxious Test Oath. From 1693 to 1775, both under the Crown and Proprietaries, no one could hold office in Pennsylvania who was not obliged, as an indispensable condition precedent, to take and subscribe to the following oath, which, after swearing allegiance to the reigning king or queen, goes on circumstantially to state: * * * * * "*We do solemnly promise and declare that we from our hearts abhor and detest and denounce as impious and heretical that damnable doctrine and position that Princes excommunicated or deprived by the Pope or any authority of the See of Rome may be deposed or murdered by their subjects, or any person whatsoever. And we do declare, that no foreign prince, person, prelate,* *state or potentate hath or ought to have any power, jurisdiction, pre-eminence, or authority, ecclesiastical or spiritual within the realm of England, or the dominions thereunto belonging."*

"And we and each of us do solemnly swear and sincerely profess and testify that in the Sacrament of the Lord's Supper there is no transubstantiation of the elements of bread and wine into the body and blood of Christ at or after the consecration thereof by any person whatsoever, and that the invocation or adoration of the Virgin Mary, or any other Saint, and the sacrifice of the Mass, as they are now used in the Church of Rome, are superstitious and idolatrous."*

Of course even the most callous Catholic would shrink from such an oath with horror and loathing, and though a premium was placed on apostasy and thereby the avenues of civil and military advancement flung wide open,—the Judas-like sacrilege would never enter his mind. He would prefer poverty and obscurity to dignities and wealth, if such a blistering sacrilege would be the price at which they were to be purchased. Another blot on Pennsylvania's fair escutcheon is the fact that only Protestants were permitted by the Provincial laws to hold land for the erection of churches, schools or hospitals, nor

---

* Stillé—*Religious Tests in Provincial Pennsylvania*, pp. 29-30.

could any foreigner be naturalized unless he was a Protestant.*

For this anomalous and inconsistent status of Catholics Penn was in no way responsible. He was the sworn champion of religious liberty, and this in the face of the most vehement opposition. Nor did he ever swerve for a moment in his advocacy of principles which he must have realized would eventually prevail. His intentions were so transparently pure that only the blindest bigotry impugned them. His intuitions, in the line of conduct mapped out in pursuit of liberty of conscience, seemed visionary and chimerical under the trying circumstances in which they were first proclaimed, but his unerring faith in the justice and wisdom of his cause must have foreshadowed the consummation that in the course of time would eventualize. His mild but unshaken faith on this subject exposed him to misconception and denunciation. He was stigmatized as a Papist, a Jesuit, a pupil of St. Omer, an emissary of the Pope. Could Penn have pursued his own mapped-out course, untrammeled by trans-Atlantic influences, unhampered by the hereditary prejudices of his subjects, he would have effectually silenced the low mutterings of disaffection stirred up by his humane conduct, and lived to see his one sublime idea an accomplished fact.

---

* *Ibid.*, p. 15.

Unhappily in the charter granted to Penn by Charles II, which invested him with well nigh plenipotentiary powers of government, both civil and ecclesiastical, an ambuscade was laid for him in Section VII, by which all laws enacted by the Provincial Assembly must receive the approval of Privy Council in England, which reserved for itself the right of adopting or repealing them for a space of five years.

It was this veto power of the Privy Council in addition to the sectarian bias that frustrated the most chivalrous, wise and humane effort ever made to give to every man the indefeasible right of worshipping God according to the dictates of conscience, a tolerance that has since its adoption been an exhaustless channel of spiritual grace and civic virtue and patriotic strength to our country.

As we intimated above, it was not until 1776 that the War of Independence gave us both civil and religious liberty, and by some strange irony of fate, the first civil office ever held in Pennsylvania, was held by a priest, and he a Jesuit, Father Ferdinand Farmer, who by an Act of Assembly reorganizing the College of Philadelphia, in 1779, was appointed a Trustee of the institution,—the Act describing him "as the Senior Minister of the Roman Churches in Philadelphia."*

That the above assertions are borne out by historic

---

* Stillé—*Religious Tests in Provincial Pennsylvania*, p. 39.

evidence, we will glean from a few data gathered at random to prove that the Catholics in colonial times simply could not make the rapid strides in social life, business prosperity, civic preferment, military achievement, educational advancement, as his more fortunate Protestant neighbor, and this owing to adverse circumstances beyond his power of control.

"He who is known here as a Roman Catholic," says Acrelius, "is hated as a half-devil, but he who has no religion is just as much esteemed for it, as though he thereby showed himself quite rational."*

The pious, humane and tolerant Penn himself was coerced by so strong and aggressive a pressure against his Catholic subjects, that at least ostensibly to silence the rasping clamors of bigots, he was compelled to write to James Logan, his colonial Governor, July 29, 1708, "There is a complaint against your government that you suffer public Mass to be said in a scandalous manner."† He subsequently recurs to the same subject: "It has become a reproach to me here with the officers of the crown, that you have suffered the scandal of Mass to be publicly celebrated."‡

The pious zeal of the holy missionaries in reclaiming the Indians from heathenism and savagery to Christianity

---

* *History of New Sweden*, (Penna.), p. 352.
† *Mem. of Hist. Soc. of Penna.*, vol. II., p. 294.
‡ Watson's—*Annals of Phila.*

and civilization,—an act of heroism, that was accomplished by jeopardizing their lives, is attributed to treasonable designs, and at once they become objects of suspicion. When Father Molyneux was acting as interpreter for the Indians of the Six Nations at Lancaster during June and July, 1744, the following accusation is at once formulated and circulated. "It is *certain* that at the time of our treaty with the Indians of ye Six Nations at Lancaster, Father Molyneux, ye principal of our Jesuits, was with them and there is grave reason to suspect that he went there for no other reason than to dissuade ye Indians from making peace with us." On his return to Maryland he was arrested, only to be honorably discharged with these grudging words of rehabilitation, "The council called Mr. Molyneux before them and after having examined him privately, discharged him without any public mark of resentment."*

The first Catholic we encounter in Cumberland County is under the ban. Governor Sharpe, of Maryland, in his communications with Governor Hamilton, of Pennsylvania, as early as 1750, speaks of a Mr. Campbell, who lived in Shippensburg, as a dangerous man, being "a Roman Catholic, and on that account likely to sympathize with the French." Though Governor Hamilton replies that "there is one Francis Campbell who was said

---

* *Maryland Memorial to the Earl of Halifax.*

to have been bred for the church among Roman Catholics, but he has the character of an honest, inoffensive man, and it is not likely that he concerns himself with the French."* All the same, Francis Campbell was an attainted man in the eyes of his neighbors, an object of espionage and suspicion.

In 1754 a society was established in Philadelphia, called the German Society, by such patriots and sober minded citizens as Dr. Franklin, Rev. Dr. Muhlenberg, patriarch of the Lutheran Church in this country, and the Rev. Dr. Smith, provost of the College, with the sole object in view to establish schools for the children of German settlers on the frontier of the Province, where they might be taught the knowledge of God, and be made loyal subjects of what was termed "The Sacred Protestant Throne of Great Britain," and thus be saved from "the machinations of French and Popish emissaries."†

In 1754 Dan. Clause warns Governor Morris of Pennsylvania against a certain man as a very dangerous character —"for he was seen making his confession to a priest in Canada."‡

In the following year, 1755, five Justices of the Peace in Berks County, sent a most alarming manifesto to the Governor of Pennsylvania, asking his immediate inter-

---

* *Penna. Archives*, vol. II, p. 114-115.

† Stillé—*Religious Tests in Provincial Pennsylvania*, p. 38.

‡ *Penna. Archives*, (Old Series), vol. II, p. 176.

vention "to enable us by some legal authority to disarm or otherwise disable the Papists from doing any injury to the other people who are not of their vile principles, * * * for in the neighborhood of the chapel (Goshenhoppen) it is reported and generally believed that thirty Indians are lurking with swords and guns and cutlasses. * * * The priests at Reading as well as Cussahoppen [old name of Goshenhoppen] last Sunday gave notice that they could not come to them again in less than nine weeks, * * * whereupon some imagine that they've gone to consult with our enemies at Fort Duquesne."* Although the Provincial Council tries to disabuse their minds and calm their fears—by telling them "that there is very little foundation for their representation," — and although the Catholics in the entire county only numbered *88*,—their anxiety was hardly allayed, and the stigma on their Catholic brethren certainly not effaced.

In the same year Governor Morris writes to Governor Dinwiddie of Virginia concerning the helpless condition of the country in the event of French invasion, that the enemy "might be strengthened by the German and Irish Catholics who are numerous here."† The latter is evidently alarmed, though the Catholics scattered over the vast territory hardly amounted to fifteen hundred, including women and children,—yet he replies reassuringly

---

* *Col. Records*, vol. VI, p. 503-533.   † *Penna. Archives*, vol. II, p. 390.

that "in the next session they will seriously consider the dangers we are in from the German Roman Catholics, and make some alteration in your constitution."*

The alteration came in due time, and placed our Catholics in a still more embarrassing, not to say distressing, situation. It was the celebrated "Act for Regulating the Militia," passed by the Provincial Council, March 29, 1757. The Act provides that a census be taken of all persons fit for military duty, except "religious societies or congregations whose tenets and principles are against arms, and all Papists or reputed Papists." It goes on to state that "no Papist or reputed Papist shall be allowed or admitted to give his vote or be chosen an officer of the militia within any of the districts within these provinces." * * * * "Every male Papist or reputed Papist, (on account of his exemption from performing military duty) between the age of seventeen and fifty-five years—must pay the sum of twenty shillings."†

In the same year—1755—an article in an English paper, reproduced in an American journal, gives a true and unvarnished description of the real status of Catholics in the Colonies and the feelings entertained about them. "But I carefully observed," the writer goes on to state, "that no Roman Catholick in our Colonies, can claim the particular privileges, thereby allowed to others; and indeed no

---

* *Penna. Archives*, vol. II, p. 423.   † *Penna. Archives*, vol. II, p. 120.

surer groundwork could be laid for the loss and destruction of our Colonies than to encourage the resort of Roman Catholicks thither."*

In 1758 Christian Frederick Post, a Moravian minister, in a speech made to the Indians at Logstown on the Ohio, thus attacked the "papists": "My brothers, I know you have been wrongly persuaded by many wicked people, for you must know there are a great many Papists in the country in the French interest, who appear like gentlemen and have sent many runaway Irish Papist servants among you, who have put bad notions into your heads, and strengthened you against your brothers, the English."† Even the mind of the Red Man was to be poisoned against the Catholic, who at all times was his only friend and benefactor.

Wealth was hardly within reach of the "papist," unless he went to the unbroken frontier. In the cities and larger towns it was not to be thought of. In 1769 John Cottringer and Joseph Cauffman asked for "An act to enable them to hold lands in this province." It was summarily refused because "the persons mentioned in this bill are Roman Catholics." ‡

It was not until the convention met in Philadelphia, in May, 1787, comprising among its members two Catholic

---

* *Penna. Gazette*, July 17, 1775.
† *The Olden Time*, vol. I, p. 116.
‡ *Col. Records*, vol. IX, p. 596.

patriots, Thomas Fitzsimons, of Philadelphia, and Daniel Carroll, of Maryland, that at the suggestion of Charles Pinkney, of South Carolina, in the face of clamorous protests, the obnoxious religious test oath was abolished, and the VI Article of the Constitution adopted, "*that no religious test shall ever be required as a qualification to any office or public trust.*" Only after years of forbearing patience, petty prosecution and enforced privations, all the time exhibiting the most indisputable and pathetic evidences of loyalty to the cause of order and freedom, was this sacred right common to humanity, secured, respected and enjoyed.

In the march of progress and prosperity, however, the Catholic was far in the rear. The most productive land had already been taken possession of, the remunerative offices, civil or military, had long been filled, and from the lowest round of the ladder, amid rebuffs, discouragements and almost insuperable difficulties, with laborious toil he had to climb to success.

Even now, however, living and breathing the atmosphere of liberty, the priesthood could hardly claim an immunity from persecution. The priest was still a curiosity to be watched and feared, no more to be tolerated than the small-pox or cholera. In our own Cumberland Valley we find this anti-Catholic epidemic raging at times in a most violent form, as virulent as it was in 1894. Father Farmer was obliged to visit the bedsides of the sick and dying in the attire of a Quaker,—and in many instances confine his travels to night only. From 1764, when the holy Father Schneider was obliged to pay surreptitious visits to his scattered flock in the disguise of a peripatetic physician, his life at times in peril, to 1795, when Father Brosius * was obliged to flee from our neighboring town, Chambersburg, pursued by a hooting and infuriated mob, and only saved himself from bodily injury by the fleetness of his horse,—the brooding spirit of persecution cropped out again and again. Nor can we, at the end of the nineteenth century, in the fierce light of modern progress and scientific achievement, boast of an ameliorated condition of affairs, as far as Carlisle is concerned.

Thus we see the incentive for Catholics to settle in the States, the prospects for bettering their condition,—the pleasing hope of civil liberty and the absence of religious persecution, were not precisely the most encouraging and alluring; added to this the deprivation of all the consolations of Holy Church, which only the Catholic can realize and feel, we are not surprised that in spite of the enticing placards posted conspicuously in villages and towns of the European Continent † to inveigle Irish and Germans to hasten to the new Eldorado, they failed to come in great numbers until the War of Independence.

---

* *Life of Gallitzin*, by Brownson, p. 99-100.

† *Eine Reise durch einige der mittleren und südlichen ver. Staaten*, Dr. Schopf, p. 90, *Schlozer's Briefwechsel*, II, No. 40.

Then suddenly the Catholics sprang into prominence, and the gallant and invaluable services rendered by a Lafayette, Kosciusko, du Portal, Pulaski, du Coudray, among the French, a Colonel Moylan, Captain Jack Barry —"Father of the American Navy," Colonel Doyle, Capt. Michael McGuire, among the Irish, and the rank and file of sturdy soldiers among the Germans, are emblazoned in the history of the country and treasured in the hearts of all patriots.

CHAPTER II.

CUMBERLAND COUNTY. — HISTORY OF THE COUNTY. — CARLISLE. — FIRST SETTLERS.

Cumberland County was the sixth in chronological order erected in the Province of Pennsylvania, and was in territorial extent the largest. The three original counties of Philadelphia, Berks and Chester, having been established in 1682, Lancaster in 1729, and York in 1749. Cumberland was separated from Lancaster by the action of Governor James Hamilton, as will be seen from the provision of the Assembly, Jan. 27, 1750 : "That all and singular lands lying within the Province of Pennsylvania, to the westward of the Susquehanna, and northward and westward of York, be erected into a County to be called Cumberland." Its southern limit was the dividing line between Maryland and Pennsylvania.

This geographical apportionment gave the county more than two-thirds of the Province. Until the formation of the adjoining counties of Bedford in 1771, Northumberland in 1772, Mifflin in 1789, Franklin in 1784, and Perry in 1820, its history is that of the whole western half of the Province of Pennsylvania.

The prominent and important part it occupies in colonial history; the thrilling scenes enacted here during the Indian wars; the patriotic share it took in the War of Independence is a matter of history, and is not our province to enter upon. Suffice it to say that at one time, especially during the Valley Forge campaign, it was a pivotal factor in the War of Independence.

The natural beauties of the Cumberland Valley, the fertility of the soil, the vast woodlands, the abundant streams, the ever-varying scenery, especially the summer and autumnal splendors, have been enjoyed by generations and elicited rhapsodical pictures from the mind of the poet, while even the cursory observer could not fail to be charmed. Encircled by the great Appalachian mountains, which skirt it like a natural fortification from the Susquehanna to its extreme southern boundary, it has, not inaptly, been compared to the sunny vale of Rasselas. In prehistoric times it was the battleground of the warlike Iroquois and Algonquin, celebrated in Indian legend and story. Later the adventurous and exploring white man entered the territory to inquire into its resources for trade.

In the Indian and Revolutionary wars it was the centre whence issued successful expeditions for the extermination of the one enemy and conquest of the other.

Carlisle, the county seat, named after the town of Carlisle in England, is situated eighteen miles west of Harrisburg, one hundred and eighteen from Philadelphia, and one hundred and seventy-eight from Pittsburgh. Its location is most admirable and picturesque, nestling as it does in the very heart of the beautiful valley. The site of the town was selected "because the place is convenient to the new path to Allegheny, now mostly used, being at a distance of four miles from the gap (Croghans) in the Kittochtiny (Blue) Mountains. * * * * the lands on both sides of the Conodoguinet are thickly settled. As the lands are settled it should be thought a proper situation for the town." In compliance with this petition Gov. James Hamilton sent a letter of instruction to Nicholas Scully, Surveyor General of the Province, to lay out the town. The letter is dated April 1st, 1751.

FIRST SETTLERS.

The first settlements made west of the Susquehanna were in the limits of what now constitutes York County, by Germans, about 1725. They were shortly followed by the Irish. The influx of German emigrants was so great even then as to arouse considerable alarm lest eventually the colony would endanger the interests, if not the existence, of the English speaking colonists. The relations between the two nationalities were never friendly, and in time became more strained. The stubborn pertinacity and phlegmatic cynicism of the one, the exasperating wit and innate pugnacity of the other, produced at best an armed neutrality, interrupted by occasional collisions and outbreaks that necessitated vigorous governmental interposition. Nor did these racial animosities abate in time nor grow less in acrimony. The attitude of the Germans and Irish continued so belligerent that an enforced separation was imperatively demanded and brought about by confining the former to York and the latter to Cumberland County. The racial amalgamation seemed impossible, and in 1750 the Proprietaries "in consequence of the frequent disturbances between the Germans and the Irish, gave orders to their agents to sell no lands in either York or Lancaster Counties to the Irish, and also to make advantageous offers of removal to the Irish settlers * * * * to Cumberland County, which offers being liberal were accepted by many." * Both submitted to law only when its majesty was invoked. In the meanwhile all seemed to live in an exciting time of "luxurious outlawry."

Many, if not the majority of these settlers came with roseate prospects and attenuated purses. Many were indigent to a degree that obliged their indenturing them-

---

* Rupp's *History of Lancaster County*, p. 288.

selves as servants for three or four years; many could not pay the twenty shilling tax imposed on servants and had to effect their landing by stealth. Many again were literally inveigled by the most Eldoradean promises of conscienceless agents, who scurried through Germany and Ireland and brought the unfortunate victims here only to find themselves sold as bondsmen to the highest bidder. These poor wretches were called "Redemptioners"; their marketable price was usually ten pounds (£10.) and the term of servitude from three to four years. The Rev. G. Muhlenburg, speaking of these German "Redemptioners," says: "When the Germans arrive here from their ships, all who cannot defray the expense of their passage from their own means must sell themselves and their families, enter a term of service to pay off their passage; such persons are called servants. After they paid their passage and earned something in addition, they emigrate up the country and make purchases."* This passingly as a possible solution why we find so many German and Irish "intruders" (squatters) on unpurchased Indian lands, and why the names of so many Catholics, who, with the exception of those in Maryland, were among the poor, cannot be found in early records, such as tax lists, etc.

The early settlers in the Cumberland Valley were the

---

* *Hallische Nachrichten*, p. 54, quoted by Rupp—*History of Dauphin* and other Counties, p. 45. See likewise Schlozer's *Briefwechsel*, IV. no. 40; *Reise durch einige der mittl. und südl ver. Staaten.* Schöpf, (Erlangen, 1788).

Scotch-Irish Presbyterians. They came in such numbers, with such resources and formed such a compact body, that their ascendancy to this day, with a few qualifications, is as unquestioned and incontestable as it was one hundred and fifty years ago. They were a persistent and aggressive element, clannish and thrifty, with all the native sturdiness of character, not altogether untinctured by illiberalism. This more by way of characterization than depreciation. For the "papists," small in number and of no helpful influence, they had more the feelings of secret commiseration than positive ill will. Even this inherited tendency of another country and other influences, was mellowed and softened in time when Catholic and Protestant stood shoulder to shoulder to battle against English aggression. If sporadic attempts to fan the dying embers of religious bigotry were attempted from that day to the present moment of writing by a ministry contracted in its views and uncharitable in its utterances, the outbursts were rendered innocuous by a healthy sentiment of justice and fair play among the laity. The gutter-smelling harangues of "converted priests" and the salacious morsels dealt out by "escaped nuns," ecclesiastical ammunition of another time and country, evoked nothing but feelings of silent scorn or condign denunciation. Even the frantic tirades against Catholic loyalty and patriotism find their amplest refutation in the forty odd flags annually unfurled on Memorial Day in the modest little cemetery adjoining the church. A mute, but none the less pathetic spectacle, are the graves of these patriots!

During the many years of the little St. Patrick's church's existence, it all the same owes much to the sympathetic, encouraging and helpful bounty of our non-Catholic citizens, and the little congregation was never chary in making its grateful acknowledgements.

The tide of emigration was so strong between the years 1725-1735, and with such avidity was the land taken up regardless of the rights of the Indian, and with such Cromwellian volubility were the Holy Scriptures quoted against the "heathen," that the Proprietaries gave Samuel Blunston a commission as agent, dated January 11, 1733-34 to grant licenses to the settlers, and to take up lands west of the Susquehanna. These licenses were mere permits to take up land and cultivate it, with the understanding that possession and a clear title should be given, when the Indians' claims had been satisfied.

The Maryland Catholics by this time came up the Susquehanna; the incoming vessels poured out streams of emigrants. As early as 1730-31 with the Indian still dwelling in their midst, and nothing but his trail to guide emigrants, they pushed westward; every available acre of arable land is taken; "clearings and burnings" are made, and the first settlements formed. The Irish and Scotch settlers locate in the Kittochtiny Valley (North Valley),

Falling Springs and many other places. In 1729 according to the *Pennsylvania Gazette* there arrived in New Castle 4500 persons chiefly from Ireland; and at Philadelphia in one year 267 servants were sold to serve a term of three or four years."

CHAPTER III.

EARLY CATHOLIC SETTLERS. — THEIR THRIFT AND PATRIOTISM.

Evidence is at hand that before 1745 a number of Irish Catholic families settled on the Tuscarora Path (Path Valley) and formed the nucleus of a settlement still in existence, and in which we not only find lineal descendants of the original settlers, but a community which in spite of the vicissitudes of time, the frequent depredations of the Indian, the great distance from a church and the sadly few visits of priests, the Catholic faith is still found as firm and intact as was that of the holy ancestors who planted it more than one hundred and fifty years ago. This settlement not only was the one that lay further west than any hitherto attempted on this side of the Alleghanies,—but even antedates as far as documentary evidence goes Conewago.

Conspicuous among these was Thomas Doyle, who on Nov. 29, 1737, took up 530 acres of land, part of which is still in possession of some of his lineal descendants. The area of land he takes on a Blunston license seems to give color to the surmise that he must have been accompanied by sufficient hands to partially cultivate it, and since he had no neighbors* a settlement of some pretension had evidently been effected. In the lapse of a few years we encounter the names of Felix Doyle, presumably a relative of Thomas, Patrick O'Neill, Shields, McMullen, Logan, who all located there before 1744.

The Doyle family enjoyed considerable prominence, as may be inferred not only from its landed possessions, but even more from the conspicuous and patriotic part it subsequently played in Revolutionary times. The town of Doylesburg, Franklin Co., is named after this family and possesses a substantial brick church dedicated to Our Blessed Lady, Refuge of Sinners, where Holy Mass is offered up monthly, it being a mission attached to Chambersburg. It scarcely admits of a doubt that this colony was the first in what then constituted the extreme West of Pennsylvania.†

In July 2, 1750 Richard Peters reports to Gov. James Hamilton, that a number of "intruders" (squatters) among whom was Henry Gass, living on Sherman's Creek (Little Juniata) six miles over the Blue Mountain (in the present Perry County) had erected log cabins on Indian lands. With others he was obliged to give a bond of £500 that "he would depart and never return," his cabin being first

---

* *History of Franklin Co.*— J. F. Richards.
† For the above information the writer is indebted to Mr. F. X. Deckelmayer, Chambersburg, Pa.

burnt to the ground. He as well as Benjamin Gass were Catholics, and after the dispossession settled in Falling Springs. He is presumably the father of Patrick Gass, who was born at that place June 12, 1771, and who was one of the first white men to make an overland trip to the Pacific, a detailed account of which he gave in *A Journal of the Voyage and Travels of a Corps of Discovery* (Pittsburgh, 1807). See likewise *The Life and Times of Patrick Gass.*

Another Catholic pioneer of whom we have information is Francis Campbell, of Shippensburg. Gov. Hamilton replying to inquiries of Gov. Sharpe of Maryland about one Francis Campbell whom he suspects of disloyalty "being a Roman Catholic, and on that account likely to sympathize with the French," allays his fears by replying that "there is a Francis Campbell who was said to have been bred for the church among the Roman Catholics, but he has the character of an honest, inoffensive man, and it is not likely that he concerns himself with the French."*

. . . Of this Campbell all traces are lost, he must have removed from his uncongenial surroundings, where his faith was not only a stumbling block in the way of his material prosperity, but exposed him to the petty annoyances and wanton espionage of his neighbors, not even escaping the surveillance of the chief executive of the Province. The other family of Campbells in Shippensburg were then as they are now strict adherents of the Presbyterian church.

---

* *Penna. Archives*, Vol. II, pp. 114-5.

Among the earlier Catholic inhabitants of Carlisle we find the Pendergrass family, who no doubt were among the pioneer settlers in the borough, and whose name will be found identified with almost all the larger settlements west of Carlisle. In Kline's *Carlisle Gazette*,* we ascertain that Philip Pendergrass died Nov. 17, 1797, "in the seventy-second year of his age, and was an old inhabitant of this borough." This Philip Pendergrass is no doubt the same, whose name is found on the list of Taxables† in 1762, and who again took part in the expedition to Kittanning‡ in 1756, to repulse the Indians, whose bloody massacres at this time sent a thrill of alarm along the entire frontier. It was of this Pendergrass family,—Garret Jr., who in Feb. 1770, while a resident of Raystown (Bedford) purchased the ground now occupied by Alleghany City, from the Six Nations. A copy of this quaint conveyance is found in Egle's *History of Pennsylvania*.§ This last Pendergrass was no doubt the same alluded to in Gov. Hamilton's correspondence with Gov. Sharpe, in which he is mentioned as being an innkeeper, thoroughly reliable and capable as a guide, and with a most minute knowledge of the topography of the country.‖

The old Pendergrass homestead was on Pomfret street, near Hanover. The house now occupied by the family, opposite the rectory, was built in the last century by

---

* Nov. 29, 1797. † Wing—*Hist. Cumb. Co*., p. 61. ‡ *Ibid.* p. 54. § p. 366.
‖ *Penna. Arch*, Vol. II, p. 114.

another Catholic family named Byrns, who intermarried with the Pendergrass's. This home, still in a good state of preservation, was built from logs cut and hewn on the premises, it being part of a dense piece of woodland. The families have both long since drifted away from their ancestral faith, and recall it only as a tradition. One of the last members of whom we have any knowledge as dying in the faith was Johanna Pendergrass, who departed this life July 9, 1823, and attached to whose death notice in the Parochial Register we find these touching words: "*Mortua est in odore sanctitatis, pietatis et devotionis;*"—" She died in the odor of sanctity, piety and devotion." No doubt a most deserving eulogy. The name of James Pendergrass is found as late as 1843 in the Parochial Records, but no evidence is at hand to prove that he died a Catholic.

The names of John and Charles McManus are found contemporaneous with the foregoing. As early as 1762 John McManus has a place on the list of Taxables.* Charles McManus, who died on August 29, 1798, was not only one of the oldest, but most progressive and successful business men in the community. The large and commodious home he erected on East Street, which still remains as a monument of post-colonial massiveness, spaciousness and solidity, with its marble slab conspicuously placed in the second story, bearing the date of its erection, 1797,

---

* Wing—*Hist. Cumb. Co.*, p. 62.

and the name of its builder, gives evidence not only of
enterprise and wealth, but cultured taste. Originally he
was proprietor of one of the largest distilleries in the
county and amassed a sufficient competence to permit him
to live, if not in luxury, at least in ease and comfort.
The avocation he followed was not then, as it is now,
looked upon as debasing and immoral : but then it was
universally adopted and countenanced as a most lucra-
tive business. As late as 1835 more than eighty distilleries paid taxes in Cumberland County alone and
manufactured more than a million gallons of whisky annually. Cumberland County always had a *penchant* for
good whisky, and the consumption of ardent spirits was
always in proportion to the output, if reliance can be
placed on local tradition. After the death of Mrs. Mary
McManus (born 1703, died December 15, 1809), at the
patriarchal age of 103 years, the name becomes less
prominent, although that of Charles is still found on the
pew rent list as late as 1823. The descendants drifted to
Mexico and Philadelphia. The former branch of the
family in the course of time founded the prosperous and
famed banking firm of McManus & Co., an institution of
international reputation and the largest and most prominent in our sister Republic. The Philadelphia family
likewise achieved more than ordinary success in life.

Jeremiah Sullivan and James Costello were two Catholics
who effected a settlement in Carlisle about 1774, and came

with resources and intentions to locate permanently. No
doubt the excitement and anxiety attending the war made
Philadelphia and its adjoining towns anything but an inviting place at this period. Cumberland county being on
the frontier afforded rare opportunities for the acquisition
of desirable land, which could be purchased for a mere song.
On March 20, 1775 * they purchased of Charles Queen
(Quinn) in Rye Township " a certain improvement
and tract of land claimed by virtue of said improvement, and situated in the Township aforesaid, bounded
by land of Samuel Murray, (Little Juniata) a claim
of Robert Steele and others containing 100 acres,
more or less." Like the Cerfoumont tract, this was in the
present Perry County. The Declaration of Independence,
the success of the Continental Army, no doubt made them
yearn for the friends they left at Philadelphia, and in a
short time James Costello's departure was followed by that
of Sullivan. It appears in the meantime Sullivan had acquired sole possession of the land. Perhaps knowing the des-
titution of the Carlisle parish, (it hardly could have escaped
his attention,) he concluded to leave the land to the church,
to form the nucleus of a small endowment which in the
course of time, would perhaps be of benefit to the congregation, as well as to its pastor. At all events Sullivan deeded
this property to Father Pellentz† in fee simple, to
hold it for the Carlisle Church. The proximity of

---

* Rec'd Bk. G, Vol. I, p. 288. † Oct. 24, 1785

this land to the Cerfoumont tract—only about four miles distance, gives weight to the presumption that the former was likewise held by Father Pellentz. That the Sullivan gift was beneficial to the church and added to its revenues, we can learn from the letter of Bishop Carrol to Rev. Mr. Debarth.*

Father Zocchi was the bearer of this letter to Father Debarth, and his receipt is still on hand. "Received from Rev. Mr. Debarth 120 dollars, for the purpose of providing a part of the salary for the attending pastor of the Catholic congregation of Carlisle, this day the 1st. of December 1807."   ZOCCHI, Pastor of Carlisle.

The land was subsequently sold by Rev. F. X. Brosius to Anthony Shattot† for £238 10 s. This occurred on April 27, 1802. This sum was converted into bonds bearing interest and left in the custody of George Metzger Esq. of Carlisle. In a letter dated 25th May 1811, the latter speaks of some funds collected on notes due Rev. Mr. Brosius, and explains that he paid various sums to Rev. Mr. Zocchi, understands that the interest on the money is to go to the support of the officiating clergyman of the "The Roman Catholic Congregation of Carlisle." He holds at the time $95.00 in hand, also judgement-bond $285.03 which he holds for the use of the "Roman Catholic Congregation of Carlisle."

These bonds, as Mr. Metzger receipts show, were given

---
* Dated Washington Oct. 7, 1807.   † Chateau, Rec'd. Bk. I. Q. p. 103.

to Bishop Carrol. Among the attorneys papers we find:
"Received from Rev. Mr. Marshall three bonds from Anthony and Michael Shatto to the Rev. F. X. Brosius, and by him assigned to the Right Rev. Dr. Carrol. Each bond bearing date 27 April, 1802 and conditioned for the payment of £21, each on the first day of April 1810, 1811, 1812."

GEO. METZGER, *Att'y at Law.*

How long the revenues went to the church cannot be ascertained. And since there appeared to be some difficulty about the title, and perhaps the trustees being more than ordinarily, if not officiously solicitous, Sullivan who had long since left for Philadelphia, made out an affidavit, dated Philadelphia, Jan. 7, 1817.*

With this, all traces of the bequest are lost, and though careful search has been instituted, no information could be obtained.

The Jeremiah Sullivan here alluded to is no doubt the

---

*" The undersigned Jeremiah Sullivan does hereby certify, that the tract of land in Rye Township. Cumberland Co.,Pa· was given by him and his partner James Costello towards the support of the Rev. Pastor attending the Roman Catholic Congregation of Carlisle and by no means to be at the disposal of any trustee or layman of said Congregation. The above tract having been sold by Rev. Mr. Brosius successor and heir to the Rev. M. Pellentz, the money resulting from the sale of said plantation ought to be laid out for the same purpose above specified in the manner the successor of the Rev. Brosius at Conewago Church thinks is most to the advantage of the Rev. Father of Carlisle."

JEREMIAH SULLIVAN.

Acknowledged by J. S. before Alderman,
JOHN GEYER, Philadelphia.

one whose name occurs so frequently in the annals of St. Mary's Church, Philadelphia (Records of the A. C. H. Society, p. 264, etc.), whilst James Costello is identically the same who in 1793 bequeathed all his property, with the exception of a few private bequests to St. Mary's Church, Philadelphia, among other purposes, for the maintenance of a school, to keep a supply of oil for the "lamp which burns in the old Chapel in Willing's Alley" (Rec'd. A. C. H. Society, p. 390) etc.

In chronological order the Faust family comes somewhat later, but was more prominently and efficiently identified with the prosperity and vicissitudes of St. Patrick's congregation, for more than fifty years, than probably any other single family up to recent times. It was a family in which a high order of intelligence was always coupled with a fervid piety, an active zeal with an undemonstrative charity, and a sterling faith with a most exemplary conduct. The ideally Catholic life of this family has not only been a heritage religiously preserved by its descendants down to the last bearers of the honored name, but it never failed to be a source of edification to their brethren in the household of faith, whilst the lofty spirituality was a revelation to those outside of the fold. To Jacob Faust, as well as John Faller, Sr., who came several decades later, the words of St. Clement, the Martyr-Pope, can most appositely be applied, when he says:* "Who is not struck

---
*I Epist. Corinth.

with beholding your lively faith: your piety full of sweetness: your generous hospitality: the holiness which reigns within your families: the serenity and innocence of your conversation?" The family must have settled here shortly after the Revolutionary War, with the Lechlers, no doubt related to the Philadelphia and Lancaster families of the same name. Eventually they intermarried with the Lechlers, though the Lechlers seemed not to possess the vigor and vitality of faith that characterized the Fausts, for they gradually strayed from the Church, though seldom affiliating with the sects. Valentine Faust, a printer, died suddenly and rather mysteriously on April 17, 1811. He was a son of John Faust, Sr. John Faust, Jr., was married to Miss Eliza Fetter at Harrisburg, November 20, 1812.* Jacob Faust, who was so conspicuous a factor in the growth and development of the congregation, enters upon the scene of church activity about 1820, and till his death was one of the great benefactors of the church, and one of the most helpful allies in keeping alive the faith at a period when priestly visits were of intermittent occurrence, and urgent pressure was brought to bear in weakening the faith of the small congregation. At the present there survive three of his children, the Misses Mary and Lizzie Faust, Carlisle, and A. J. Faust, A.M., Ph.D., of Washington, D. C.

---

* *Carlisle Gazette*, November 26, 1812.

The Schwartz family must likewise be enumerated among the pioneer stock. One of the oldest monuments in the cemetery, in fact the oldest decipherable, records the death (in quaint German) of Nicholas Schwartz, who died August 23, 1784, the year in which the log chapel was built. The monument is a pretentious one for the time in which it was erected, and is not only in a good state of preservation, but will last a century or two more, unless ruthlessly broken or mutilated. Tradition has it, that he was a Hessian officer, captured at the Battle of Brandywine or Trenton, and brought here as a prisoner to the barracks. He espoused the cause of the Revolutionary party, did active and gallant service in the cause of Independence, and was universally esteemed as a good citizen and brave soldier. The name was subsequently anglicized to Black, and figures in the church records as late as 1823.

Michael Dawson must have settled here shortly after the Declaration of Independence, and in 1798 was the possessor of considerable farming land in what now belongs to Perry county. He attained more than local prominence as a builder and contractor and was in good circumstances. James Dawson "while employed in erecting the penitentiary or work house in the gaol-yard, was suddenly killed by a falling scaffolding,* June 15, 1815.

---

* *Carlisle Volunteer*, June 22, 1815.

Michael Dawson was a candidate about the same time for sheriff, but failed to secure the nomination by a piece of political jugglery that would have done no little credit to the adroit achievements of modern politics. The family a few years later moved into Cambria county. Both were soldiers in the war of 1812, and the former, as far as known, was probably the first soldier buried with military honors in our cemetery.

The absence of all church records covering this period precludes all possibility of ascertaining with any degree of certainty, the names of other Catholics perhaps prominent in their day, who may have settled in Carlisle or Cumberland county and who perhaps yielded to none in zeal and generosity. Unfortunately until that historical treasure trove—the Conewago Baptismal Record, and that of its affiliated missions is unearthed, we must content ourselves with the fragmentary data and names perpetuated by the court records and local history.

In this connection, it would be a most fascinating study to trace the vestiges of Catholic missionary labor among the original owners of the land—the Indians. It is more than an assumption, that the ubiquitous and irrepressible Jesuit, whether of Canada or Maryland, had long since not only studied Indian customs, but acquired their language, and gained many a joyful spiritual conquest long before the white man, with the implements of civilization,—oftener those of war, drove them from their old haunts. The kindness with which the French always treated the Indians, the integrity displayed in their petty commercial transactions, the respect they entertained for their national customs, above all the intense eagerness and loving condescension of the Jesuits in attending their spiritual welfare, made a lasting impression on the untutored child of the forest. There can be little or no doubt, that Canadian missionaries at some period or other had visited the Indian settlements, especially those bordering the Susquehanna River, where a number of Catholic Indians dwelt. Moreover the interchange of tribal courtesies, and the fealty owing by an immemorial custom to the chieftains, makes the visits to Canada on the part of the Pennsylvania Indians more than a mere presumption. Again there is direct evidence, that the most prominent chiefs in Pennsylvania in the early colonial period, were then, or had been, members of the Church.

Foremost stands the imposing and heroic figure of Shikellimy, the Oneida chief, one of the most august and impressive characters found in colonial times, who at this period resided at Shamokin (Sunbury). A man of fearless intrepidity and dauntless courage, he yet had the ingenuousness of a child and the heart of a woman. His transparent honesty, uniform kindness, unquestioned truthfulness, and instinctive love of justice, makes him stand in bold relief, as the diametric opposite of what legend and history usually ascribe to his race. The

Moravian missionaries can hardly find fitting terms to convey their exalted opinion of the transcendent virtues of this man, whose love of justice and truth was so great "that he was never known to violate his word or condone an offense." The *Colonial Records* are ineffaceable eulogies of Shikellimy, whose name always inspired reverence and awe. According to the Moravian missionaries he was baptized in Canada by the Jesuits, and always wore "an idol" on his breast, no doubt a blessed medal. He died at Bethlehem, in 1748, having followed the Moravian missionaries to that place. He was the father of the eloquent Sajechtowa, better known as Logan, the Mingo chief, whose famous address is known to every schoolboy.

Another prominent character, who figured in colonial history, was Madame Margaret Montour. In early life she married Roland Montour, a Seneca brave, and at his death Carandawana, chief of the Oneidas. She lived along the Susquehanna as early as 1727. She was a woman of masculine mental and physical vigor, and ruled her people with an autocratic sway, in bold contrast with that of the mild Shikellimy. Her influence was of a nature, that made not only traders, but even colonial governors court her grace, with an assiduity and obsequiousness, half amusing,—had it not been essentially necessary. Her allegiance to the English was but half-hearted, and at times extremely dubious, if not suspicious, for, of French extraction herself, she could not forget the kindness of which she and her adopted people had been the recipients. She was held in such high esteem that when her husband Carandawana was killed in a war with the Catawbas, Thomas Penn, then Proprietary, saw fit publicly to express his condolences to her.* The settlement she founded was variously called Ostonwakin, "French Town," or "French Margaret's Town," and was situated on the area covered by the Seventh Ward (Newberry) in Williamsport. When Count Zinzendorf, the Moravian missionary, first called on her, thinking him a French priest, her joy was great, for now she could have "her child baptized." Her loyalty to her faith and to the French, both of which seemed synonymous terms at this period, caused no little irritation and fears to the government. Montour county, and Montoursville in Lycoming county, are named after Madame Montour.†

French Margaret was a niece of Madame Montour, and was likewise famous in her day. She was the first prohibitionist of whom we have any record in Pennsylvania. She had prohibited the use of liquor in her little village and claimed her husband, Peter Quebec, had not drunk rum for six years.‡ In 1754 French Margaret and her Mohawk husband, and two grandchildren traveling in

---

* *Hist. West Branch.* By McGinness, p. 102.
† *Memorials of the Moravian Church*, p 320, et seq.
‡ *Hist. West Branch*, p. 135, (foot note.)

semi-barbaric state, with an Irish groom, and six relay and pack horses, emigrated to New York.

Andrew Montour, whose name is always coupled with that of Conrad Weiser, is another name figuring frequently and prominently in the colonial history. He was the son of Madame Montour, and acted as interpreter for the English. Whether he remained steadfast in the Faith is extremely doubtful. In 1755, he lived on a grant of land (800 acres) given him by Gov. Hamilton in 1752, ten miles northwest of Carlisle, between the Conodoguinet, a creek near Carlisle, and the mountain. He was naturally of a roaming character, and freebooter-like sold his services to the highest bidder, though the *Colonial Records* bear evidence to the invaluable services he rendered the government, and the extremely hazardous missions he undertook in conveying despatches, etc. However, one moment we hear that the French set a reward of £100 on his head, and shortly after he leads a band of warriors in capturing the Gilbert family in Lehighton.

From these random citations it will be seen that thorough historic research in this unexplored field would yield some strange and astonishing data. Some future historian, with ready access to the Jesuit Relations and Canadian church records, will no doubt throw light on this hazy subject, and prove that before the Catholic white man set foot in Pennsylvania, his Catholic brother of the household of Faith had already glorified God in his own simple, but none the less fervent and Catholic manner.

CHAPTER IV.

PIONEER PRIESTS—REV. JAMES PELLENTZ, S.J.—HIS LARGE PARISH—HIS HEROIC EXPLOITS AND ENDURING MONUMENTS.—FIRST VISITS TO CARLISLE.

One of the most illustrious champions of our holy religion, a pioneeer in laying the foundations of Catholic settlements, a veritable apostle in the magnitude and fruitfulness of his labors, was Rev. James Pellentz, S.J. He was not only one of the forerunners of Catholicity in Pennsylvania, leaving an honest fame and precious memory wherever he set foot in his extensive wanderings, but one of the actual founders of St. Patrick's Congregation. To him next the Providence of God, the Cumberland Valley, York and Huntington Counties, in short the whole of Western Pennsylvania and Maryland owes a debt of undying gratitude. In his unflagging zeal and consuming love of souls, he stands pre-eminent as an ideal priest; in his austere virtue, inexhaustible patience, unwearied charity and invincible courage, he was a typical son of St. Ignatius; in his quick apprehension and almost intuitional knowledge of the eventual growth, development and prosperity of the new country, he proved himself the hopeful, unerring patriot. The record of his indefatigable zeal, his extensive wanderings, his childlike faith and his burning charity, recalls and compares favorably with the brightest pages of missionary toil and achievement in this country. When the history of the Catholic Church in Pennsylvania shall be written from better authenticated sources than the fragmentary and scattered data, which necessity compels us to accept now, the name of Pellentz will receive its due measure of recognition and eulogy, and hand it down to coming generations in prayer and benediction. Time will only add to its lustre.

Rev. James Pellentz, S.J., was born January 19, 1727, in Germany; entered the Society of Jesus in 1744, and made his vows in 1756. He was sent to this country from England in 1758 with Rev. James Augustine Frambach and two other Jesuit fathers.

REV. JAMES PELLENTZ, S.J.

According to Treacy* he spent ten years in Lancaster, Pa., and a year and a half at Frederick Town, Md., before he assumed charge of Cone-

---

* *Old Catholic Maryland*, p. 177.

wago. In all probability he was sent to Conewago and from there attended Lancaster as circumstances demanded. At all events, like the apostles of old he was not to confine his labors to one city or community, but the scene of his forty years' activity was to embrace an entire country, the whole of Pennsylvania, west of Philadelphia. Never was missionary more ardent in his zeal, more cheerful in his sacrifices, more hopeful in trial nor courageous under persecution, than this stranger in a strange country, speaking a strange tongue. From our modern standard of measuring heroism, his position seems simply to have risen to the unattainable.

Old settlers were accustomed to relate, not without a glow of admiration and a heart swelling with gratitude, how this holy priest traversed the whole country, penetrating every settlement and clearing, even crossing the Alleghanies in search of the scattered Catholics, whom stress of circumstances obliged to seek this enforced isolation, *on foot.** If we bear in mind that this country was still infested by the Red Man, that in territorial extent the missions covered more than a hundred and thirty miles, that the bridle path or Indian trail, was frequently the only road that could be traveled, (the new military road of 1755 was still almost impassable), that the luxury of bridged streams was as yet unknown, that shelterless nights and exhausting days were more the rule than the

---

* *St. Vincenz in Penna.*, p. 56.

exception,—and bearing in mind that in addition to this Father Pellentz carried all the requisites for saying Holy Mass,—the altar stone, missal, vestments, chalice, etc., in a bundle strapped to his back, we leave the reader to draw his own picture of this missionary in his holy wanderings.

Every rude hut would serve as a temple, every improvised table as an altar. The manger at Bethlehem was fully as decent as many places where the Unbloody Sacrifice was offered up.

It took the first wagon that went West in 1789, drawn by four horses from Hagerstown to Brownsville, more than two weeks to get to its destination. The progress made by a solitary traveler on foot in 1758, weighted with a heavy burden and at times faint from fasting, is a picture worthy of a poet's pen or painter's brush.

Pennsylvania is marked with the footprints that attest his pious zeal, and dotted with landmarks that give incontestable evidence of his prudent foresight. For it must be borne in mind that the whole State of Pennsylvania from the Delaware to the Ohio was territorially apportioned to but five priests at this time. Revs. Robert Molyneux and Ferdinand Farmer (Steinmayer) were stationed at Philadelphia; Luke Geissler, of whom we will presently hear again, at Lancaster; John B. De Ritter, at Goshenhoppen, and James Pellentz at Conewago.

In his apportionment Father Pellentz had the whole of Pennsylvania west of the Susquehanna as his parish.

The magnitude of the task, the inaccessibility of the settlements, the hardships and privations of travel did not dampen his zeal; for what were these difficulties compared to the poignant sorrow of seeing souls perish for want of spiritual nutriment? The number of Catholics was pitifully small; their mode of life for obvious reasons not gregarious, and consequently they were scattered promiscuously if not fortuitously wherever an asylum was offered from religious persecution or marauding Indians. As late as 1784 the census of souls gives us this startling revelation of the number of Catholics under the Proprietaries: Philadelphia and adjoining counties—*one thousand;* Goshenhoppen, seven hundred, and Conewago and missions only five hundred. These five hundred were scattered from the Susquehanna to the Ohio, the only known Catholic settlements being Conewago and Path Valley,—with an increasing population in Carlisle, Shippensburg, Huntington and Bedford (Raystown). What now comprises New York State had not one church, and the city which then was the capital of the country, had only eighteen communicants of whom three were Germans, and no nationality ascribed to the others.

The following letter written by one of his companions, his sacristan,* may lift the veil and give us a passing glimpse of the arduous toil and sore hardships that formed

---

*Mainzer, *Monatschrift von Geistlichen Sachen,* (1785), p. 457; quoted by Reily in his *Recollections in the Life of Cardinal Gibbons,* p. 563.

the routine life of Father Pellentz. It is an excerpt from a letter written to a German magazine by Paul Mueller, dated June 28th, 1785 : "Oh that the good God would be merciful and send us energetic spiritual advisers, what grand harvests they could make. Our good father James Pellentz, who is nearly fifty years of age, and twenty-eight in this country, has very much labor day and night, with sick calls, confessions and sermons, especially on Sundays and Holy Days, when, from six o'clock in the morning till twelve and one o'clock, he hears confessions ; so that it is usually from two until half past two, before the Holy Mass is over, and often, with baptisms and sermons, it is after four o'clock before he takes any nourishment ; and often he has weak spells at the altar, and then (meaning after Mass) one or two are waiting to take him on sick calls. From this one can judge how many confessions he has to hear, when I, who make for him all the Hosts he uses, have made from March 24th until today, June 28th, 2740 small hosts that he used. From this you can see what an enormous labor for one man."

The prudent counsels and rare executive ability of the good father no doubt had much to do in adjusting the national animosities, and his thorough knowledge of the country's topography stood him in good stead in forming our coreligionists into more cohesive and compact bodies, and as a nucleus to insure the perpetuation, he wisely purchased land for churches. The Catholic once resting under the shadow of the cross ceases to be a nomad, fells the trees, clears the land, tills the soil, erects his log cabin, and establishes his home.

CHURCH OF THE SACRED HEART, CONEWAGO, PA.

In 1784 he sent Father Geissler, his assistant at the time, money to purchase a house at Carlisle "to hold service in," of which we shall hear more presently; in the same year he secures a building at Littlestown for the first church in that community; in the same year he paid £31 for a church site at Standing Stone, the present Huntington. In 1785 he began and finished the massive stone structure, which has the enviable distinction of being the first church erected in honor of the Sacred Heart in this country, at Conewago. He improved the place by the erection of a commodious and substantial parsonage, with the necessary adjuncts indispensable at that time—a capacious barn and extensive farm buildings. In 1786 he was one of the main factors in the establishment of Georgetown College, and was appointed one of its directors. In 1791 he was one of the attendants at the First Provincial Council of Baltimore, and was appointed Vicar General by Bishop Carroll. He was likewise one of the promoters and subscribers to the first Catholic Bible published in this country in 1789, it being a reprint of Bishop Challoner's revision, issued from the press of Mathew Carey.

Human activity and physical endurance could not hold out long under the ravages of such rigorous and incessant toil; the inadequacy of the laborers, the vast extent of the vineyard, the inclemency of the weather and the climatic changes, could not fail but undermine the most rugged health and daunt the most courageous spirit. It was the crying demand for more help that not only urged him to make frequent appeals to Germany for priests, but found him ever ready with the necessary funds to defray the expenses of the wearisome and certainly not inexpensive voyage. Father Pellentz himself writes, under date of Aug. 20th, 1785, in a letter forwarded to Coblentz on the Rhine: "I pray you do everything in your power to send me two priests to America. Since my last letter affairs have gone considerably worse here, as our dear Father Luke Geissler is at present so weak that we fear he cannot live long. I myself have also a fever which oppresses me greatly, and from all appearances will render me unable to continue my great labors that I have until now undergone. * * * I have a flourishing mission and from the number of those who receive the Blessed Sacrament, there is no other in the whole of North America which will compare with it. It is a great pity that we have not more priests. They could bring back to the right path many who have strayed away, since we now have full religious liberty."*

In 1795 we find Father Pellentz at Port Tobacco, Md., and the newly ordained Prince Demetrius Gallitzin as his most capable and efficient assistant.

After forty years of arduous, but fruitful labor,—laying the foundation of Catholic faith in Pennsylvania, he went to his eternal reward on Nov. 21st, 1799, dying at Cone-

---

* *American Cath. Hist. Researches,* July, 1891. Vol. VIII, p. 132.

wago, where his remains were interred, and where this beautiful epitaph commemorates his holy career:

> "REV. JACOBUS PELLENTZ SECURUS MORITUR, FECIT SE
> MORTE RENASCI
> NON EA MORS DICI, SED NOVA VITA POTEST
> NOMEN PELLENTZ ISTE TERQUE QUATERQUE MORETUR
> HOSPES! UBI JACIT HIC ET DOMUS ET DOMINI
> TEMPLUM! QUODQUE SUUM FECIT ZELO PIETATE
> UT POPULUM TENEAT SUB GREMIO ECCLESIAE."

("Rev. James Pellentz dies in peace by the grace of Him who by His death regenerated him. Not death, but rather life should it be called. The name of Pellentz has many claims to consideration. A stranger in a strange land, he erected this the temple of God, and with zeal and piety made it the object of his life to gather men within the Church.")

It falls to few men to make and leave such a noble record. His work will forever remain a monument of zeal, determination and genius. His purity of life, goodness of heart, pervasive efficacy; his discipline and labor in the church; the breadth of his knowledge, the grandeur of his ideas concerning the future of the church in this country, form together a combination of characteristics worthy of the most glowing pages in the history of missionary achievement.

CHAPTER V.

REV. CHARLES SEWALL, S. J., ATTENDS CARLISLE.—ATTENDS THE MISSIONS ATTACHED TO CONEWAGO.—MAKES THE FIRST PURCHASE OF PROPERTY FOR A CATHOLIC CHURCH IN 1779.—FIRST RESIDENT PASTOR OF BALTIMORE.—HIS LABORIOUS LIFE.

The next priest of whom we have definite and tangible evidence in Carlisle, is the Rev. Charles Sewall, S. J., an assistant to Father Pellentz, imbued with the same zeal, inspired by the same charity and rewarded by the same results. No doubt the latter had taken more than a casual survey of the territory that composed his parish, discerned the possibilities that lay hidden in the different towns and settlements, and at the proper time adopted the necessary measures to effect purchases which eventually would lead to the formation of parishes and construction of churches. The unobtrusive and efficient manner in which the former carried out the designs of his superior, the methodical plan adopted in the formation of these different charges, and the generosity with which they were assisted and maintained, gives but another evidence of the total absorption of self in the apostolic work before them. In this formative state of society the poverty of the faithful precluded all possibility of their making purchases either of land or property, therefore the priest came not only with an open heart to minister to their spiritual wants, but with an open purse to supply their material resources. The first sites for churches, and the first churches were built without entailing any pecuniary responsibility on the faithful. The court dockets give ample testimony of this truth.

Where did the financial aid come from ?

The Society of Jesus was suppressed in 1773, its members exiled from Catholic countries, while only Prussia under Frederic the Great offered an asylum—"to preserve the seed," as he facetiously writes to Voltaire, "that he might at some time furnish it to those who should desire to cultivate so rare a plant."

The Empress Catharine likewise invited them to Russia and gave them charge of the four colleges respectively at Polotsk, Vitepsk, Orcha and Dimabourg. Flattering and honorable as these acts may have been, they certainly were not remunerative, nor adequate to supply the individual wants much less the increasing expenses of the missions.

It is probable, in fact strong presumptive evidence is at hand, that the support of these missions was derived from an endowment made by Sir John James of Heston, Middlesex, England. By its provision £4000 was held by the Vicar Apostolic of London, with the proviso, that forty pounds be annually applied to the Catholic poor of London, the balance to support the indigent missionaries in Pennsylvania. It was regarded as annexed to the church at

Lancaster, and for many years gave twenty pounds annually to four missions in Pennsylvania. Was Carlisle one of these?*

Rev. Charles Sewall, S. J., the actual founder of the Carlisle parish was born in St. Mary's County, Maryland, July 4th,† 1744, on his father's estate at Mattapany on the Patuxent River. He came from good old English stock. His ancestors came from England with Lord Baltimore in 1634, and of course were devout Catholics.

The environments of his childhood, the atmosphere of piety in which he spent his boyhood, the association and intercourse with the holy men who then ministered to the spiritual wants of the Catholics throughout the broad domains of Maryland and Pennsylvania, could not fail but make a forceful and salutary impression on the mind of the susceptible youth. The church of St. Nicholas adjoined his father's estate, which was but twelve or fifteen miles from St. Inigo's, one of the sacred landmarks of Catholicity in Maryland,—attended then as it is even now by the fathers of the Society of Jesus.

It is very likely that he made his preparatory studies at Bohemia Manor, a seat of learning which the Jesuits had established in spite of penal laws. He entered upon his collegiate course at St. Omer's in France, in 1758, when

---

* *Am. Cath. Hist. Researches*, Vol. V, No. 4.
† *The Cath. Church in the U. S.* De Courcy, p. 543.

but fourteen years of age. In 1764 he entered the Society of Jesus; and returned to this country with Father Augustine Jenkins, S. J., on May 24, 1774.

His first mission was one to tax the most perfervid neophyte. As we saw above, a perilous ministry if not self annihilation awaited the priest in those days. To traverse nearly the entire State of Maryland and Pennsylvania on foot, on horseback or in ram-shackle stage coaches in quest of the few persecuted, poverty stricken Catholics was a physical ordeal of no small magnitude; to live on the charity of the poor, sharing their rude log cabins and homely fare, was to this man of gentle birth and cultivated tastes a labor of love,—for was not the Son of God born in a stable, where there was but scant comfort, and died on the cross where there was none? Cruel arrogance, coarse insult, haughty defiance, bitter menace and inextinguishable hatred confronted the missionaries at almost every step;—but with uncompromising firmness, with gentle speech and invincible courage they toiled and prayed and persevered until the harvest for which they planted the seed though unreaped and ungarnered by them, was still showing promise of a golden fulness to their eager views.

It was such a destiny that awaited Father Sewall when he assumed his position as assistant to the saintly Pellentz at Conewago. Lancaster, York, Elizabethtown, Chambersburg, Carlisle, Huntington, Bedford, not to mention the widely scattered missions in Maryland, were the theatre of this man's zeal.

The hardship, exposure and privation of such a life, not to dwell upon the "*solicitude for the churches*" threatened to cut short his active career, and his health caused his superior no little concern and anxiety. A change of climate, and a life different from that of an itinerant missionary was necessary. From 1782 to 1793 we find him in charge of St. Peter's Church, Baltimore, Md., being the first resident pastor of that city. From a letter of Father Pellentz to Dr. Carroll we glean the following: "I am entirely satified with Mr. Sewall's resolution to stay in Baltimore, as I always thought he would not live long here, and that he would do more for God's greater glory and the salvation of souls in Baltimore than here. For that reason I advised him in his trouble to have patience and to take courage. To the same intent I called to his remembrance that Saints Ignatius and Theresa expected always great success when they met with serious obstacles in the beginning of a new college or monastery. The hardships Mr. Sewall suffered made me think that Baltimore would be a very flourishing mission. I beg of your Reverence not to be uneasy for keeping Mr. Sewall from me. I am fully persuaded that he is more necessary where he is than here."*

---

* Rev. J. Pellentz to V. Rev. Dr. Carroll, Feb. 27, 1786.

His career in Baltimore did not disappoint the hopes centered in him. His labors extending over ten years were rewarded beyond his most sanguine expectations, and the prophetic foresight of Father Pellentz as to the religious possibilities that lay hidden in Baltimore more than verified.

Though a man of scholarly attainments, a versatile linguist, a profound theologian, a capable business man,— his success as a pulpit orator seemed hardly to rise above the level of respectable mediocrity.*

This was more than ordinarily disappointing to the poor father, living as he did in a community where all the niceties and graces of oratory had been cultivated as of paramount importance by the Protestant ministry. However this deficiency in no way affected his usefulness, nor the impression he left on his people. A man whose austere, pure life, could not escape the observation of even the unthinking world—was the most persuasive of sermons in itself. When eventually Dr. Carroll took up his home with him in 1786, and his own simple, unctuous efforts were inadvertently pitted against the transcendent eloquence of one of America's most luminous intellects and most magnetic orators, the line of demarcation being more conspicuous than ever was not disheartening or depressing to him. Full of sweetness and charity, he still continued unremitting in his holy work.

---

* Scharf—*Chronicles of Baltimore*, p. 251.

Every enterprise to ameliorate the condition of his people and further the ends of Holy Church found in him a ready advocate and a gallant champion. Whether it was his missionary excursions through Pennsylvania from 1774 to 1792, or his presence at the First Synod of Baltimore in 1791, or when he acted as one of the incorporators of Georgetown College in 1786, or temporarily supplied Bohemia Manor in 1793, or acted as agent for the Corporation of Clergy in 1797, or built the church in St. Thomas Manor in 1798, or was one of the first to re-enter the Society of Jesus upon its restoration in 1802,*—he was ever active and eager in the service of God, ever ready to assume any work allotted to him. He worked on modestly and unobtrusively,—one unerring and deep searching Eye alone penetrating his heart and soul, seeing its secret motives, reading its unpublished thoughts, divining its unrevealed desires.

His health never robust was rapidly failing under the strain of incessant labor, and on Feb. 25th, 1805, he writes to his brother, Father Nicholas Sewall, S. J., who on the restoration of the Society of Jesus entered the English Province, "that for six weeks past I have been confined to my room and unable to say mass, but I hope to be able to officiate in the church next Sunday." Whether his pious wish was gratified we cannot ascertain.

---

*Bp. Carroll to Fr. Marmaduke Stone, Balto., 1805.

On the following tenth of November, 1805, he surrendered his soul to God at St. Thomas Manor, where no doubt he was buried.

The fact that he was assistant to Father Pellentz implied that his parish embraced the Province of Pennsylvania, and we can trace his career as far as Standing Stone (Huntington), where he suggested the advisability of having his superior purchase a place to hold service in, which was actually done in 1785, when he paid Rev. Luke Geissler £31 with this object in view. There can be little doubt, that like his superior he penetrated even the remotest missions and settlements that were in the vast territorial jurisdiction of Conewago. In doing so, like the prudent and farseeing observer Father Sewall was, he could not fail but detect the possibilities that lay hidden in the embryonic towns, which in the Providence of God might become important and populous cities, in which the Church of God, might become a factor of soul-saving importance in the promotion of virtue and holiness, and concurrently, thrift and prosperity. Therefore we see that unaided, though no doubt encouraged by the pioneer settlers, he, and especially Father Pellentz, made a careful survey of the advantageous lands and eligible sites that were constantly in the market, purchased them and thus laid the foundation of the future parish. In many enterprising localities free sites were offered for churches, conditioned upon an obligation to erect a church within a specified time,—this evidently more to be an encouragement to colonization than a promotive inducement to morality.

Carlisle as a bustling frontier town, the centre of considerable commercial activity, with abundant educational facilities,—one of the main arteries that carried traffic west, south and east,—not to mention the increasing and highly progressive population, could not fail but create the hope that the future had promising realizations in prospect. No doubt fully impressed with these sentiments, Father Sewall on the 5th Feb., 1779, on one of his periodic visits, made the following purchase in Carlisle:

<small>Deed
Robert Guthrie
the younger
to
Charles Sewall</small>
This Indenture* made the fifth day of February in the year of our Lord one thousand seven Hundred and seventy-nine Between Robert Guthrie the younger of the town of Carlisle, of the County of Cumberland and State of Pennsylvania, joiner of the one part, And Charles Sewall of Heidelburg Township of the County of York and State aforesaid of the other part Witnesseth that the said Robert Guthrie for and in Consideration of the sum of Thirty Pounds Lawful Money of Pennsylvania to him in hand paid by the said Charles Sewall at or before the execution hereof the receipt and payment whereof is hereby acknowledged, and the said

---

*Dated Feb. 5, 1779, *Record Book E.* p. 304.

Charles Sewall thereof forever acquitted and Discharged by these Presents, he the said Robert Guthrie Hath granted, Bargained, Sold, Released and Confirmed and by these presents Doth grant and Bargain, Sell and Release and Confirmed unto the said Charles Sewall and to his Heirs and Assigns a Certain Messuage and Lott of Ground Situate and being in the Town of Carlisle in the County of Cumberland aforesaid. Bounded on the North by Pomfret Street on the East by a Lott the Property of Robert Cummins on the South by a Twenty feet alley and on the West by a Lot of Robert Guthrie the Elder Containing in front on the said Street Sixty feet and in Depth to the said Alley two hundred and forty feet. Known in the General plan of the said Town by its No 274 Together with all and singular Buildings and improvements thereon and Premises with the appurtenances whatsoever thereto belonging or in any ways appertaining and the Reversions and Remainders Rents Issues and Profits thereof and all Estate Right Title Interest Property Claim Demand Whatsoever both at Law and in equity of him the said Robert Guthrie of in and to the same and every part thereof. To have and to hold the said Messuage and Lott of Ground hereby granted and released or meant mentioned or indented so to be with the appurtenances unto the said Charles Sewall his Heirs and Assigns. To the only proper use benefit and Behoof of the said Charles Sewall his Heirs and Assigns for ever Subject to the Quit rents due and to become Due to the chief Lord of Lords of the fee and the said Robert Guthrie for himself and for his Heirs Doth hereby Covenant promise grant and agree to and with the said Charles Sewall his Heirs and Assigns by these presents that he the said Robert Guthrie and his Heirs the above Mentioned and Described Messuage and Lott of Ground with the appurtenances unto the said Charles Sewall and his Heirs and all and every other person or persons whomsoever lawfully Claiming or to Claime the same or any part thereof from by or under him the said Robert Guthrie and his Heirs shall and will warrant and forever Defend by these Presents. In Witness whereof the said parties to these Presents have hereto interchangeably set their hands and Seals the Day and year first above Written.

Signed Sealed and Delivered   Robert Guthrie
in the Presence of   [SEAL.]
   John Gray
   Jno. Steel junr.

                     Received the Day of the Date of the above Indenture from the above named Charles Sewall the sum of Thirty Pounds Lawful Money ass'd being the full Consideration therein Mentioned. Witness my hand the same day and year first above written.

   Witness present
   JOHN GRAY   ROBERT GUTHRIE
   JOHN STEELE, Junr.   [SEAL.]

Cumberland County, *ss.*

Be it remembered that on the fifth Day of February, Anno Domini 1779 Before me the Subscriber one of the Justices of the Peace Assigned &c to keep &c came the above named Robert Guthrie the Younger and acknowledged the above Indenture to be his act and Deed and Desired that as such the same may be recorded. Witness my hand and Seal the day and year above written.

JOHN CREIGH.

Received March 5th 1779 and compared with the original. WM. LYON, Recd.

The location was then considered, if not a most eligible one, one that at all events had some commendable features, prominent among which was its cheapness. The culture and wealth of the town clustered about the Public Square, and scattered itself over High and Hanover Streets. It was the centre of professional and commercial life, the churches, the inns, the public square, were then to be found as they are now, within a stone's throw of the old seat of justice. However, East Street had some substantial if not pretty homes, which indicated not only thrift and comfort, but independence, and no doubt Pomfret Street may have had possibilities from a speculative point of view, very satisfactory to the investor. Moreover a purchase of property for Catholic worship would possibly have encountered some opposition should its aspirations have been to enter the more prominent streets. The church was still looked upon with a disdain not untinged with suspicion and fear. Even the prospect of a remunerative investment may have been counterbalanced by the latent bigotry, which made the Catholic more an object of *vigilant* tolerance than that of a pure patriotism which respected his rights as an equal. The second barrier in the way of going up town, and perhaps the more convincing one, was the depleted exchequer of the poverty stricken missionary.

Here then, three years after the Declaration of Independence, ten years before the Constitution had been framed, with authority still vested in the Supreme Executive Council, with General Washington in command of the Continental forces, Benedict Arnold in command of the military at Philadelphia, Lieut. General Sullivan carrying a war of extermination into the country of the Six Nations, Colonel Brodhead heading a most successful expedition up the Susquehanna against the Muncy towns, with the country divided into clamorous Tories and bellicose Royalists, with no national currency as yet in sight, the first foundation of Catholicity, west of the Susquehanna, was laid.

CHAPTER VI.

REV. LUKE GEISSLER, S.J., BUILDS THE FIRST LOG CHAPEL IN CARLISLE, 1784.—NEED OF GERMAN PRIESTS.—PURCHASES A HOUSE IN HUNTINGTON TO HOLD SERVICES IN.—CARLISLE CHURCH THE ONLY ONE BETWEEN LANCASTER AND ST. LOUIS.—REV. STANISLAUS CERFOUMONT.—HIS HISTORY.—VERIFICATION OF AN OLD TRADITION.—REV. LOUIS DE BARTH.—ERECTION OF FIRST BRICK CHURCH AT CARLISLE 1806.

The next priest of whom we have any authentic information as being closely identified with Carlisle, and who belonged to that zealous band of Catholic pioneers, whose work and foresight now elicits our admiration, as it no doubt earned the gratitude of their contemporaries, was Father Geissler. Like the former he belonged to that intrepid band of Conewago Jesuits, whose labors were as incessant as their presence was ubiquitous, when souls were to be saved and God glorified. To their admirable tact, consistent prudence and uniform harmony which guided them in their scattered labors and which permeated the little society on the frontier of civilization, may be ascribed much of the success and certainly the perpetuity of their efforts.

Rev. Luke Geissler, was born in Germany in 1735, entered the Society of Jesus in 1756, became a professed father in 1772. He landed in Philadelphia on March 26th, 1769. For a number of years he made his home with Father Pellentz as an assistant, and from Conewago as the centre missionary work radiated, reaching every known Catholic settlement, even family in the Province.

At this time the urgent need of a German priest was more keenly felt,--not only on account of the increased emigration, but in Carlisle on account of the recent accession to its population by transferring many of the captured Hessians to this frontier town. For after the capture of Trenton Dec. 25th, 1776, a large number of these poor Hessians were sent to Carlisle, and were employed in the erection of the stone military barrack, a part of which are still in existence.

Out of the 16,992 that were hired to England by Landgrave Frederick II of Hesse Cassel, although almost all Protestants, not a few Catholics were to be found, who no doubt were loth to return to the life of serfdom, when such glorious prospects of liberty were within reach. In Philadelphia alone more than six hundred were married,[*] in many instances to Catholics. At all events the fact that only 10,402 returned gives strong color to the presumption that many deserted and settled down in America. Out of the Carlisle prisoners no doubt many, pitied and treated with great kindness by its citizens who realized the

---

[*] *Records of the Am. Cath. Hist. Soc.*, Vol. II, p. 300.

unwilling role they played in the War of Independence, preferred to share the hopeful future and promising anticipations of this country to the certain penury and servitude of a bankrupt petty German principality. Our cemetery gives evidence that some of them either by birth or conversion were Catholics, and their bodies lie interred in consecrated ground.

In 1784 Father Geissler was sent to take charge of St. Mary's Church, Lancaster, then known as the Mission of St. John Nepomucene. It was shortly after he assumed charge of this parish, that he must have built the first log chapel which tradition mentions, and which was then commonly known as a "Mass-house," located about midway between Pomfret St. and what on account of the building, has ever since been known as "Chapel Alley." As usual in establishing new churches the faithful were not called upon for financial aid, and the money for the lot on which the building was erected, as well as the building itself was advanced by the missionaries.

The chapel was no doubt long in contemplation, and its erection, modest, plain and ungainly though it was,—a consummation ineffably sweet to the Catholic heart. Its presence was an assurance that now, regular spiritual ministration was in prospect, and that at least Holy Mass might be celebrated in a house, which belonged to Our Lord alone. Father Pellentz writes to Very Dr. Carroll from Conewago under date of Oct. 1st, 1785: "I paid Mr.

Geissler ninety-six pounds (£.96) for a house in Carlisle to keep service in ; thirty-one pounds (£.31) for a house in Standing Stone bought with Mr. Sewall's advice."*

The structure must have been of a most unpretentious kind, and furnished to meet only the most pressing needs of the people, the priest making his abode as usual with some of the faithful. The temporary character of the structure must have been very much in evidence,—for the influx of Catholic emigrants, the growing prosperity of the old settlers, the more tolerant attitude of Protestants, and especially the increasing prominence of Carlisle,—would hardly warrant these prudent clergymen to imagine for a moment that the primitive structure would not be soon supplanted by a more worthy edifice. No trace or vestige of the old chapel remains. Only a remote tradition has kept alive the fact that the chapel was built of logs, and that it was situated between Pomfret Street and Chapel Alley. Death, emigration to the west, and loss of faith, have been perhaps more potent in effacing these old traditions, than the removal of the hallowed landmarks themselves.

This chapel was the first Catholic house of worship erected west of the Susquehanna. At the time of its completion it was the only building specifically set aside for Catholic worship between Lancaster, Pa. and St. Louis, Mo. In

---

* Rev. Jas. Pellentz to V. Rev. Dr. Carroll, Oct. 1st, 1785.

chronological order it ranks fifth in the State of Pennsylvania, outside of Philadelphia. The churches at Lancaster, Goshenhoppen, Conewago and York alone antedate it.

At this time there was a crying need of priests in Philadelphia. The Catholic population since the Declaration of Independence was increasing rapidly; new settlements were effected contiguous to the city; the priests were growing old and feeble, unable to cope with the engrossing cares and everchanging difficulties that cropped out at every stage of the work. Father Molyneux and Father Farmer toiled unsparingly for years, and with increasing years they felt increasing infirmities, or as the former sententiously puts it—"every day the labor increases and my ability decreases." Father Geissler himself was to step into the breach, though already feeling the hand of death. Father Molyneux writes to Very Rev. Dr. Carroll for an assistant and singles out Father Geissler.* "I hope," he writes, "you will consider us and order Mr. Geissler to our assistance if possible. It is pleasing to me, to Mr. Farmer, and he himself is sensible of the necessity. For my part I have no private views, the public good is all I seek."

To shirk duty or be dilatory in obeying orders in emergencies of such a nature are delinquencies that can seldom be laid to the charge of the priesthood,—to the

---

* Rev. R. Molyneux to V. Rev. Dr. Carroll. *Woodstock Letters*, pp. 193-94.

Jesuit never. Though suffering from a malady, which as we saw above caused considerable anxiety to his superior, Father Geissler went to Philadelphia, and with Father Beeston assisted Father Molyneux. However he remained only for a short time.—His illness assumed such a stage that he hurried back to Conewago, where he finally succumbed, dying on August 10th, 1786.*

Speaking of him and Father Farmer, Shea says—" Both were of that band of excellent missionaries whom the Jesuit provinces in Germany had sent to America to attend their countrymen, but whose labors were given unstintedly to all Catholics." His twenty years of missionary work displayed the tireless energy, the heroic courage, and imperturbable determination, that seemed to be the providential endowment of all his colaborers. Like them, his disinterested love of souls, his intrepidity in confronting the manifold difficulties that beset his path, and his triumphant assertion of divine truth "in season and out of season," were the mainsprings of action, the predominant attributes of his character. Like them, we find him identified with every religious, educational or moral enterprise that was calculated to lead men to holiness and peace. Like them, his prayers were heard, his labors blessed, and the glory of God promoted.

---

* Treacy, *Old Catholic Maryland*, p. 181.

REV. STANISLAUS CERFOUMONT.

Prominent among the missionaries who in the meantime, and early in the year 1800, did meritorious work, though his name occurs with less frequency, and seems less conspicuous than the preceding, was the Rev. Stanislaus Cerfoumont, who succeeded Father Geissler. His personality is shrouded in considerable mystery, and the avidity with which early historians took it for granted that all who were connected with the Conewago mission were on that account Jesuits, only added to the general mystification. Conewago during the first half century of Catholicity in Pennsylvania reflected and focalized Catholic life; it was the asylum of the emigrant priest, no matter to what nationality or religious order he belonged; it was the centre from which Catholic life radiated. All who came for the Pennsylvania missions, outside of Philadelphia, reported at Conewago; from there they received their instructions and credentials, and only as the accredited agents of Conewago, did they receive the respect and homage of the Catholics.

The evidence in the case of Father Cerfoumont seems to preponderate on the side that he was a Franciscan, who though he made his home at Conewago and died there, was never a Jesuit.* This we may infer from the following

---

* In reply to inquiries made by the Rt. Rev. Camillus Maes, Bishop of Covington, Ky., the Ballandists at Brussels state that the name of Cerfoumont is not found in the official records of the Society of Jesus.

letter quoted by Maes in his "Life of Rev. Charles Nerinckx." Speaking of Conewago, the letter goes on to state: "A beautiful chapel has been erected in the neighborhood by a Jesuit, (Pellentz) and in the pastoral residence I found a precious library of Flemish and Dutch books left by a Franciscan missionary of Liège, who had resided there."*

This no doubt was Stanislaus Cerfoumont, since an old tradition connects his name with large contributions to the library.† Whether he subsequently joined the Society of Jesus, is likewise a mooted point on which no light can be thrown—though in the mind of the writer it is highly improbable.

Rev. Stanislaus Cerfoumont was born in the diocese of Liège in the year 1751. Of his career, until he came to this country in 1785, little is known. Like all missionaries who entered this vineyard, he attached himself to one of the larger missions in the capacity of assistant. His field of activity was virtually the same as that of his holy companions, whose hardships and privations he shared. Traces of his itinerant career can be discovered in all the outlying missions of Conewago and Lancaster. His name is likewise found in Maryland and at the First Synod of Baltimore.

Two incidents in his career we beg to call especial atten-

---
* Maes, *Life of Rev. Charles Nerinckx*, May 6, 1806.
† McSherry, *Hist. St. Aloysius Church, Littlestown*, p. 64.

tion to. The one reads like a romance, and if it goes to establishing anything, it is the trustworthiness and veracity of local traditions.

Shortly after the writer's ordination (1877) he was assigned to Lykens, Pa., as assistant. In his parochial work he was frequently summoned to Millersburg, Dauphin Co., Pa. His intercourse with some of the intelligent non-Catholics of that community disclosed the existence of an old tradition, that at one time a priest had lived on the other side of the river in Perry County, and as a confirmation of the truthfulness of the report, it was alleged that some of his "sacred robes" were still, in a rather tattered condition, in the supposititious priest's house. There was such a delicious flavor of mystery about the narrative on the one hand that almost set an immediate investigation in progress,—but on the other hand there was such an air of romantic improbability, that the matter was left in abeyance, at least for the time being. More persistent and veracious witnesses however led the writer to make cursory inquiry before entering upon a search. A clergyman of the diocese, in whose knowledge of diocesan history it was thought implicit confidence could be placed, dismissed the matter summarily by maintaining that it was probably a vestment, "forgotten by some priest while saying Mass for the Catholics employed in the construction of canals." Our knowledge of the topography of Perry County was so childishly imperfect at the time—

that we never investigated whether the county had any canals or railroads, or like John Ruskin's ideal country was free from "these curses of modern money making traffic." At the time the opinion seemed so reasonable, that the matter was dropped.

In searching the court dockets of Cumberland County, by the merest accident, the writer to his amazement, which resolved itself into joyous gratification, discovered this deed: *

"JAMES KEENEN
TO THE
REV. STANISLAUS CERFOUMONT."

It goes on to state that on the 16th August, 1798, James Keenen of Juniata Township, Cumberland Co., in consideration of the sum of thirty pounds, Gold and Silver, sold to Rev. Stanislaus Cerfoumont of Heidelberg Township, York Co., a certain plantation and tract of land in Juniata Township, comprising one hundred and fifty acres of land, buildings, barns, stables, etc., etc.

This deed seems to be a complete verification of the "priest" and "sacred robe" tradition, both of which had an actual existence, the memory and locality of which the lapse of a century may have somewhat dimmed, but certainly not effaced. Juniata Township was located near the present village of Mifflin, Juniata County, and the priest whose history was veiled in so much exasperating

---

Deed Book, M. p. 721.

mystery, clearly revealed. Whether more Catholics than James Keenen had settled in that locality, research fails to establish. Old parishioners recall the family traditionally as being related to the Very Rev. Bernard Keenan, for more than fifty years pastor of St. Mary's Church, Lancaster.

In spite of painstaking research here and careful inquiries in Perry County, aside from the tradition, no evidence could be discovered which would lead to a confirmation that Father Cerfoumont at any time resided on this plantation, or any intimation for what purpose he made the purchase. Being a Franciscan, and it being an opportune time for the founding of a settlement, both on account of the cheapness of land and the increasing influx of immigrants, no doubt he had in view the nucleus of a Catholic settlement, not unlike Conewago, Goshenhoppen and Sportsman's Hall. The distance from the main artery of trade—the turnpike—and the unproductiveness of the soil not to allude to the inaccessibility of the place, may have frustrated all designs in that direction. The date of the purchase lends color to the surmise that Father Cerfoumont was on one of his periodic visitations, and that James Keenen, no doubt a Catholic, came to Carlisle to attend Holy Mass on the Feast of the Assumption Aug. 15th, the initiative taken then and the sale consummated on the following day.

A strange and melancholy feature connected with this

purchase is, that most minute search instituted and conducted by experienced attorneys and local historians, fails to establish a legal sale or transfer of this property. However, the work is still in prosecution and some future day may shed more light on this tradition.

The other incident fraught with so many blessings to our Catholic emigrants, was that Father Cerfoumont was the instrument in bringing to this country a man whose transparent purity of life, inexhaustible zeal, and heroic devotion to duty, not to touch upon his ripe scholarship and luminous intellect, made him one of the grandest figures in the beginning of this century and acclaims him the Apostle of Kentucky. We refer to the Rev. Charles Nerinckx, the virtue and faithfulness of whose life is fully recorded by Bishop Maes, in his interesting and edifying biography of that apostolic priest.*

It was in a letter dated Conewago, July 20th, 1801, written to his half-brother, Father Gouppi, Secretary to the Bishop of Liège, that Father Cerfoumont gave such a vivid and pathetic recital of the missionary needs of this country, that Father Nerinckx, to whose attention the letter was brought, resolved at once to come over and join the gallant band of intrepid priests, who did such invaluable service in the early church of the United States.

---

* Maes, *Life of Rev. Charles Nerinckx*.

After nineteen years of missionary labor in America, Father Cerfoumont died at Conewago, Aug. 2nd, 1804, aged fifty-three years.

REV. LOUIS DE BARTH.

The death of Father Cerfoumont, left Carlisle as before an affiliated mission to Conewago, only that now we find it occasionally attended from Lancaster. In Carlisle affairs were evidently assuming a more prosperous and encouraging aspect; success rewarded some of our Catholic settlers in business and public life; religious intolerance had lost much of its oldtime aggressiveness and virulence. The respite was a source of gratitude and thanksgiving, and the warmest expression of such a feeling was found in the new church about to be erected. The log chapel had not only outgrown its usefulness, but was no doubt a secret cause of keeping many of the vacillating spirits from attending divine service. With the growing population, there was a corresponding growing desire to have a place of worship more in consonance with the prevailing prosperity and more adapted to the service of God. The faithful, though few, were fervent; though composed of various nationalities were united; though still of meagre resources and attenuated purses, were all the more generous and self-denying. It only needed the guiding hand and controlling spirit of a capable and zealous pastor, to bring about the most sanguine realizations.

The man providentially sent to inaugurate this work, not only in Carlisle, but in all the adjacent missions, was not only adapted by nature, but endowed by divine grace to bring about the most marvelous results. A churchman in the fullest acceptation of the word ; a shrewd, keen, alert business man ;—the possessor of rare administrative ability coupled with the most engaging manners. Withal there was found in him singular concentration of patient zeal and sweet piety, that could not fail to attract, and attract only to challenge admiration and reverence. His suave and courtly manners evidenced the gentleman by birth, his holy and successful career the priest by the grace of God.

Such was the Rev. Louis De Barth, born Nov. 1st, 1764, at Munster, Germany. He was the second son of Count Joseph de Barth and Maria Louisa de Rohmer. From earliest youth he showed unmistakable predisposition for the priesthood, and the whole intellectual trend of his earlier years seems to have been a preparatory advance to it. He made his collegiate studies at Bellay in Belgium, and his theological course at Strasburg, where he was raised to the holy priesthood in 1790. The terrors of the French Revolution, forced him, as it did thousands of the nobility and priesthood, into exile. Unlike many, who were awaiting the termination of the saturnalia of licentiousness and blood, he did not go to England, the welcome home of the refugee,—but he cast his eyes about to see where a proper field of usefulness awaited the exercise of his zeal. In the fall of 1791 he came to America, and at once presented himself to Bishop Carroll for active service. Like his eminent friend and contemporary Prince Demetrius Augustine Gallitzin, who dropped the princely title to assume that of plebeian John Smith, until legal complications compelled him to resume his titular rights, so Count Louis de Barth, in consecrating his life to God, renounced his title to nobility and was known only as plain Louis Barth.

After doing brief missionary work at Bohemia Manor, Maryland, late in 1791, he was sent to Port Tobacco, May 12th, 1792, and for a few years labored in that field, which then comprised the lower counties in Maryland. In 1795 we find him at Lancaster* where according to some authorities his parish embraced the whole of Central Pennsylvania, comprising 10,113 square miles, in the most remote parts of which the meagre Catholic population was promiscuously scattered. Lancaster, with Conewago was now the centre from which missionary activity issued. Lebanon, Elizabethtown, Milton, Little Britain, Elizabeth Furnace, were some of the more prominent little towns in this vast parish, not to mention the "clearings" and minor settlements that dotted the fertile and

---

* Foin, in his Paper relating to Rev. Louis Barth. in *Records of the Am. Cath. Hist. Soc.*, Vol. II., p. 30.

inviting lowlands and rich and promising mountainous districts of Pennsylvania.

The accession of Father De Barth to the pastorate of Lancaster signalized a new era in the history of the church in Pennsylvania. A new impulse was given to religious life,—a more vigorous vitality to Catholic faith. The congregations already existing were annealed into a a more compact and concrete, and coincidentally a more energetic and assertive body; the provisional log chapels were being rapidly supplanted by substantial stone and brick structures; a more systematized mode of procedure was adopted in imparting knowledge of Catholic doctrines, by catechisation; the monthly, semi-annual and annual visitations to the various settlements opened the channels of sacramental grace; the contagion of schism and insubordination, which, already showing its malign influences in Philadelphia, was effectually stamped out by an exemplary life that commanded respect, by an eloquence that was soul-thrilling, by heroic acts of self-denial that were pathetic. With the princely Gallitzin colonizing the unbroken wilds of the Alleghanies, and threading his way through craggy defiles and tortuous bridlepaths, living in abject poverty,—but ever a ministering angel of consolation and grace to the isolated settler,—and the noble De Barth exchanging his ancestral home for the log cabin of the pioneer, leading a life of ceaseless toil and hardship in the fertile and teeming plains adjoining the

Susquehanna, one of the most inspiring spectacles in the
church history of the State is revealed to us. In the
enduring work of these two apostolic men, animated by
the loftiest ambition, fired with the most beneficent zeal,
striving for the consummation of the same eternal ends,
we have an achievement that must not only leave its
impress on the ecclesiastical history of the state, but one
that will ever be treasured in the heart of every devout
Catholic. Their deeds of heroism are still a living and
hallowed memory; the monuments wrought by their
hands still remain to attest the prudence and zeal of their
conduct, the holiness of their lives, and divinity of their
mission.

Father De Barth's eminent and commanding abilities
were of so transcendent a nature, that in spite of a shrinking
modesty he could not escape the attention of his
ecclesiastical superiors, nor shun the unwelcome applause
of the faithful. On January 15th, 1804, we find him installed
as the superior of Conewago, a position that
attached to itself both the administration of its temporalities
and spiritualities. The selection besides being a most
judicious one, was one that was soon to be made memorable
by results that surpassed the most sanguine expectations.
Until now, Conewago was in charge of the Jesuit
Fathers, which though suppressed kept up the community
life and discipline as much as circumstances would warrant.
His appointment was made by Bishop Carroll, him-

self a Jesuit, and most of his subordinates were members of the Society. Father De Barth was a secular priest. That the most implicit confidence was placed in his prudent foresight, transparent honesty and consummate administrative skill, is amply attested by the public acknowledgement recorded in the Annals of the Society of Jesus, at Georgetown, D. C., which proclaims the integrity and fidelity with which he acquitted himself in the discharge of his arduous and exacting duties.

His departure from Lancaster led to great internal dissension in that parish, which at one time assumed an alarming aspect, so that in 1806 he paid a long visit to the place, placated the rebellious Germans, and re-established peace.

It was, whilst exercising the office of administrator at Conewago, and being brought in closer touch with the small missions, that the brick church was built here in 1806, under his supervision.

The structure was still small, about 40 x 35 feet, almost painfully plain, but in any event a vast improvement on the old log chapel. All the same, the undertaking was one that must have taxed the scant resources of the few Catholics to their utmost, for now they were called upon to contribute. The structure was nondescript in style, with no architectural pretensions whatsoever. The monotony of the two lateral walls, about 21 feet in height, was relieved by four unsymmetrically large windows (two

on each side). The modest front, Quaker-like in its prim demureness, had a central entrance, flanked by two large windows. The corner stone by some inexplicable turn of affairs was placed above the central entrance, and consisted of a plain solid brown sandstone, with the Latin inscription neatly and correctly carved :
Portae inferi non praevalebunt adversus eam.
M.D.CCCVI
("The gates of hell shall not prevail against thee.")

There was no receptacle for documents, coins, etc., nor any evidence, outside of the inscription to indicate that it was to serve the purpose it did. Of the interior of the church we have no information. No doubt it had the customary plain wooden altar, plainer pews, and the historic tenplate stove, etc., etc.

How and where the funds were secured for this building is a matter of mere conjecture. Church records of that period have been destroyed, and newspaper files shed no light on the matter.

During these widely scattered missionary excursions Father De Barth had the assistance of men, all of whom left an enviable reputation for learning and piety. In fact, if we view these men in the light of intellectual attainments, we cannot fail to be surprised to find them in the wild and arid wastes of an unbroken wilderness and frontier civilization instead of filling some professorial chair in a European college or university. Father F. X.

Brosius was an eminent scientist and profound theologian. In 1796 he issued a *Reply of a Roman Catholic Priest to a Peace-loving Preacher of the Lutheran Church* (*16mo. 196 pp.); in 1813, *The Elements of Natural or Experimental Philosophy*, Cavallo-Brosius; and in 1815, *A New and Concise Method of Finding the Latitude by double Latitudes of the Sun*. It was he who gave George Ticknor his first instruction in German, preparatory to his going to the University of Göttingen.†

The other assistant was Father Gallitzin, the Russian Prince, who in joining the Church, renounced a mapped out course that would have paved the way to the highest distinctions of diplomatic or military life. The formidable and trenchant pen he wielded, the logical grasp of mind and vivid directness of style, and his thorough equipment as an astute polemic, is in full evidence in his *Defence of Catholic Principles*, his *Appeal to the Protestant Public*,— which not only summarily effected the complete discomfiture of his opponent, but have ever since, by their lucid presentation of Catholic doctrines, been of incalculable service,—translated as they were into almost every modern tongue. His life has formed the subject of a most interesting and readable volume, by Miss Sara Brownson. ‡

The other assistants were Father Egan, who was conse-

---

* Finotti, *Bibliographia*, p. 225.
† George Ticknor's *Life, Letters and Journal*, vol. I, p. 11.
‡ *Life of the Rev. D. A. Gallitzin*, by Brownson.

crated First Bishop of Philadelphia, Oct. 28th, 1810, Rev. Nicholas Zocchi* and Rev. Adam Marshall. There seems to be little doubt that all these alternated with their superior in attending Carlisle, at intervals sometimes long, sometimes short, when a sick call imperatively demanded their service, etc. The query naturally obtrudes itself—how could these men, with their manifold and fatiguing labors, their distracting and harassing duties, with no appreciable time for literary recreation or concentrated study,—how could they find time to cultivate the graces of literature, follow their bent for scientific investigation, or delve in abstruse theological problems?

In attending the missions, Father De Barth usually went on horseback, and "no one was better known or more beloved than Father De Barth, whose coming was always hailed with delight." In later years growing infirmities probably more than improved roads, made him indulge in a less exhausting, even if more dangerous and expensive mode of travel. The two following letters, now published for the first time, show the care and solicitude exercised in the construction of the conveyance adapted to these roads, which incidentally gives an insight into their unsafe and perilous condition. The first letter is addressed to the Rev. Mr. Byrne, pastor at Lancaster. No doubt like the

* Father Zocchi's knowledge of English was very defective. His vocabulary failing him one day in reciting the Litany of the B. V. M., at Carlisle, made him startle his congregation by closing the litany with some hesitancy,— "*moutons* of God, who takest away the sins of the world!" He died at Taneytown, Dec. 19th, 1845.

deacon, in Holmes' wonderful "one-hoss shay," many annoying accidents and exasperating experiences, taught him to have his conveyance "built in a logical way." It was evident he knew that—

> "There is always somewhere a weakest spot
> In hub, tire, felloe, in spring or thill,
> In panel, or crossbar, or floor, or sill,
> In screw, bolt, thoroughbrace—lurking still."

and therefore gave such circumstantial and minute instructions about this wonderful one horse gig. We produce it *verbatim et literatim :* *

"CONEWAGO, Dec. 16th, 1812.
"REV'D. MR. BYRNE:
"REV. & DEAR SIR,
"As I expect to be in Littleyork on Sunday the 24 of January may be I will come myself for the gig, you are so obliging as to procure for me. As the double joints are said to be much better than the single I give preference to the former. They may be plated if you think it best. In everything do as you would for yourself. As I am often riding on the side of hills, it would be best to have the tyres of the wheels hollow on the outside. As Mr. Brown † prefers the steel springs I

---

* The author is indebted to S. M. Sener, Esq., Lancaster, Pa., who holds the original letters and kindly furnished the copies.

† Mr. Brown was an old Lancaster carriage builder.

am perfectly satisfied to have them so and wish them now of steel.

"Rev. Mr. Neale's gig has several straps which secure the body of the gig to the running parts from upsetting when the gig leans on one side on hilly or bad roads. I saw also that the wheels are fastened to the axle-tree by a square box screwed to the axle-tree, and if I am not mistaken a pin goes thro' that box and axle-tree to keep said box from unscrewing itself.

"Be so kind also to get me a small trunk suitable for a single traveler, strong and well made, well covered, proof against rain, and two leather straps to fasten it behind the gig. The box under the seat ought to be movable and furnished with a lock and key. I forgot to mention about the harness. Brass I have been told is apt to break, iron will rust. I was advised to have them plated. This I leave to your Reverence, but have nothing done for mere ornament. I have seen some carriages here and in Europe whereof the steel springs were bound in with a rope twisted around the springs to support them, as I was told. If Mr. Brown thinks this will be of service I wish it done, the more so as I must drive thro' very rough roads, over roots and rocks, and am obliged to go carefully and slowly in such places. I could not go out of a walk for the greater part of my whole ride.

"I have seen some gigs which had no iron bond along

beneath the shafts. I think it would be best to have one on each shaft to a proper length."

"I remain Revd and Dear Sir
 Your Obedt & Humble servant
 [*Signed.*] L. BARTH.

The other letter is addressed to Anthony Hook, one of the old Lancaster Catholics and a warm friend of Father De Barth. It is dated, and runs thus:

"CONEWAGO, Feb. 24, 1813.

"DEAR SIR:

"I fully intended to get to Lancaster tomorrow, but I hear of so many accidents happening to those who attempt to cross the river on the ice, that I must give up my plans. I am to officiate at Littleyorke next Sunday, and if there be at that time no danger in crossing I will send a man and horse to take the gig. Mr. Metzger in Hanover is intimately acquainted with Mr. Swartz in your town. I will next Friday propose to him to accept from me about $360, and give me an order upon his friend Mr. Swartz, who I hope will accept it. The order will be payable to Revd Mr. Byrne or to you in his absence.

"The balance after paying the gig is for Mrs. Michenfelder and Christina.

"I don't remember if I mentioned to Mr. Byrne to procure a horse collar of a large size and a buckle to enlarge or shorten it. The horse I intend to use in the gig is a stout and able animal. God grant that I may have good luck with him.

"From Mr. Byrne's account of the gig I am sure I shall be pleased with it. I am in the greatest need of it,— after a long ride and even a short one if the horse makes a blunder I am obliged to keep my room. I am much obliged to you for the trouble you have taken in this business, and shall forever remain as I always have been" "Your sincere friend and servant

[*Signed.*] L. BARTH.

"To Anthony Hook.*"

The two preceding letters give us a passing glimpse of the missionary equipage in the early part of the century. A gig that was virtually a chapel, containing all the essentials for divine worship, such as vestments, missal, altar stone, chalice, etc., securely stowed away under lock and key; with straps securely holding the body of the gig to the running gear, to keep the trundling, top-heavy conveyance from tilting over on those perilous mountain roads that even now endanger the most expert horseman. Anyone who has travelled the highways and by-ways of the interior of the State even at the present time, especially when the "vernal sun sends teeming life through nature's arteries" will pardon the circumstantial instructions, nor smile at fears that were anything but groundless.

---

* Thomas Hook was another of Lancaster's pioneer Catholics.

On July 29th, 1814, Father De Barth was promoted, by his whilom assistant, Bishop Egan, to the position of Vicar General, and after his death, was appointed administrator of the diocese by Archbishop Carroll, to exercise "all the authority of the deceased until the Holy See appointed a new Bishop."

His mild sway, coupled with prudential insight, that seemed a characteristic attribute of his character, averted dire calamity in the diocese. The seeds of revolt had been sown, and a destructive schism was imminent,—but the tact, forbearance, magnanimity of the administrator, averted what seemed inevitable. His judicious and beneficent course as administrator could not fail to single him out as a worthy successor to the See of Philadelphia,—and though both Archbishops Maréchal and Cheverus were urgent in having him accept,—and though it is claimed the Bull of Investiture had already reached Philadelphia, he gently, but peremptorily refused to entertain the acceptance.*

His administration, extending over three years was productive of much good; his diplomacy, mild but unyielding, holding in check the clashing elements, that embittered the dying moments of Bishop Egan, and were a

---

* "I will not accept, but will kneel down and devoutly put the bulls in the fire. Then I will make out testimonials for myself signed in my real name as Vicar General and give myself another name in the body of the paper, and then farewell, Monseigneur. Neither you, nor anyone else, shall ever know the corner of the globe where I shall vegetate the few years left me to live."—V.Rev. L. De Barth, to Archbishop Maréchal, quoted by Shea. *History of the Cath. Ch.*, Vol. III, p. 222.

source of such grave scandal and irremediable harm in the years following.

After the appointment of Bishop Conwell he retired to his church at Conewago, to become again a simple country missionary. In 1828, Archbishop Whitfield (Archbishop Carroll died Dec. 3d, 1815) appointed him pastor of St. John's German Catholic Church, Baltimore. Only when the weight of years and the accumulation of infirmities, gave unmistakable premonitions that his strength was inadequate to the labors of his pastorate, with unimpaired mind, dauntless courage and undampened zeal, did he retire to Georgetown College to await with composure and hopefulness the summons that would usher him to his eternal reward. "As long as his strength permitted he never allowed a day to pass without offering up Holy Mass; and when increasing feebleness took away this solace, he received holy communion daily, till his holy death, which occurred Sunday, Oct. 13th, 1844. He died well prepared in the Lord, a good and faithful servant, in the eightieth year of his age and the fifty-fourth of his priesthood."

He died attended by his brother, General Barth de Walbach, and a few friends. The funeral took place on the 15th Oct., and his remains were interred in the cemetery belonging to Trinity Church, Georgetown, D. C., where a plain tombstone marks the last resting place of one of the most heroic types of the Catholic missionary that modern history in our country can show.

A strong personality is disclosed to us in Father de Barth, where quickness of decision, concentration of purpose and fertility of resources are most admirably blended with true depth of humility, total forgetfulness of self and an insatiate thirst for the salvation of souls. A personality that combined marvelous enthusiasm with discretion, bravery with coolness, piety without obtrusiveness, zeal without presumption,—and above all an inexhaustible charity, which no failure could dampen, no trial endanger, no disappointment extinguish. Had he accepted the bishopric of Philadelphia,—the onerous responsibility alone made him recoil from entertaining the idea,—perhaps the scandal and schism which ensued could have been averted.

CHAPTER VII.

BISHOP CARROLL REPLIES TO REV. DR. DAVIDSON'S ATTACKS ON THE CHURCH.—THE EDITOR REFUSES TO PUBLISH HIS LETTER.—CHIEF JUSTICE TANEY ATTENDS DICKINSON COLLEGE.— TOUCHING OBITUARY NOTICE ON ARCHBISHOP CARROLL BY A PROTESTANT.

Although the prevailing sentiment in Carlisle was thus far tolerant and never openly hostile to Catholics, occasional sporadic outbursts convinced them that the right of full and unimpaired citizenship was accorded them rather grudgingly by one of the dominant factors in those days—the Presbyterian clergy. There may have been a few notable exceptions,—but the uniform antipathy was so stern and unbending that they counted for little. To them the Church was still under a ban; it was still the target at which the bolts of impotent pulpit thunder, scriptural prophecy and implacable denunciation was to be hurled. The annual recurrence of the sermon against Popery was as unfailing in making its appearance, as the annual spring doses of senna as a cathartic, manna as a laxative, or sulphur and molasses as a blood purifier, with which our forefathers religiously dosed themselves. The clergy felt, or pretended to feel that the Pope, aided by some monarchic and satanic coalition, had matured plans for the establishment of the Catholic Religion in America and mentally they depicted the exodus of hundreds of dissenting ministers, ejected from their pulpits, stripped of their livings and sent to starve among the Mohawks or Iroquois on the frontier. The alarm was at times changed to consternation, when Catholicity effected a foothold in some large community, gained a convert or established a nunnery. That the children of men, brothers in Divine sonship, equal in their spiritual nature, of indefeasible right, independent of all earthly power in the domain of conscience, each of them, even the humblest and most degraded, independent in that sacred sphere, and accountable to God alone, were to be looked upon as equals, was an abstract truth that could be philosophically entertained in private, but certainly not theologically enunciated in public.

But the Church which grew like an undying plant under penal laws and ostracism, did not fail to thrive under bigotry and intolerance. Moreover the more intelligent and liberal church members, looked upon these annual attacks of sectarian rabies as they did upon the supposed hygienic perils of the dog days. They had to come, they had to be borne, they were not only innocuous, but mildly humorous. The mock heroic attitude of irascible ministers hurling bitterest defiance at a decrepit, poor, old Pope, thousands of miles away, and with gaudy phrase, specious argumentation, illimitable confidence and ebullient enthusiasm, proving that this tottering ecclesiastic on the verge of eternity, had sinister designs on the peace and liberty of this country was so deliciously ludicrous and picturesquely grotesque, as to be looked upon as a most delightful diversion from wearisome hours of expounding the sacred text. It was no doubt, more an inherited tendency, than a religiously grounded conviction that inspired these dithyrambic diatribes. But the minister had not fallen from the high estate into which Puritanism had hoisted him. He was still looked upon with some unorthodox reservations of course, as the "just man made perfect, the oracle of the divine will, the sure guide to truth,"* and when he annually attacked Popery, he was listened to with respectful awe. These annual attacks, delivered in every variety of key, from the filthy ribaldry of some contemporary Thersites to the dire vaticination of the colonial Cassandra, all heralded the approaching extinction in fire and blood of the City of God, which they found as a monster sodden in black corruption, with whom there could be no terms in the heart of a humane man.

One of the most prominent ministers at Carlisle at this time, was the Rev. Dr. Robert Davidson, who was called to the pastorate of the Carlisle Presbyterian Church in 1785, and in addition to his pastoral charge filled the professorship of history, chronology, geography and rhetoric, at Dickinson College, under the presidency of the scholarly Dr. Nisbet. The extent and profundity of his learning is unknown to us, but seemingly Catholicity, or even the philosophy of history, was a study outside the orbit of his intellectual range, and he certainly knew as much about the merits of hydrophobia as he did about Catholicity, with no doubt a preponderating inclination to study the former in preference to the latter. " He was disliked by the students generally, and some of them took'no pains to conceal it. . . . He was formal and solemn and precise, and, in short was always the pedagogue in school and out of

---

* McMaster, *Hist. of the People of the United States*, Vol. I, p. 31.

school. . . . He had written a rhyming geogra'phy, which as well as I can remember contained about fifty printed pages, printed in octavo."* This geography of which he was very vain, had to be memorized by the students, even the acrostic on his own name.†

No one but a man of such mental calibre and theological oddity, could have issued in *Kline's Carlisle Weekly Gazette*‡ the following production, whose quaint and comprehensive title we reproduce in full: " *The Signs of the Times:* " *or the Overthrow of the Papal Tyranny in France, the prelude of destruction to Popery and Despotism: but of Peace to Mankind.* By T. Bickeno (4th Edition, London) *Epitomized by the Reverend Robert Davidson, D.D.*

The epitome extends through three weekly issues and

---

* *Memoir of Roger Brooke Taney, LL.D.*, p. 42.

† *R*ound the globe now to rove, and its surface survey,
*O*h, youth of America, hasten away
*B*id adieu for awhile to the toys you desire,
*E*arth's beauties to view, and its wonders admire;
*R*efuse not instruction, improve well your time,
*T*hey are happy in age who are wise in their prime.

*D*elight'd we'll pass seas, continents through,
*A*nd isles without number, the old and the new;
*V*ast oceans and seas, too, shall have their due praise
*I*ncluding the rivers, the lakes and the bays
　　*　*　*　*　*　*　*　*　*

" *The rest,*" says Chief Justice Taney, whom we are quoting at the age of 77 years, " *has dropped from my memory.*"

‡ July 29, 1795.

covers eleven columns of closely printed matter. It certainly must have made the geography class chuckle with delight. It is a most quaint and ingenious literary and biblical production, couched in an archaic and portentous diction, in harmony with the momentous subject. Profusely interlarded with scriptural quotations, drawing liberally on astronomical, chronological and historical data to bolster up the theological manikin. The argumentation is abstruse to nebulousness. The subject itself seemed to evade all ideas of perspicacity. An evident predilection obtrudes itself of delving in metaphysical subtlety and obscure mysticism, rather than allow full play of the searchlight of honest inquiry, or be guided by the accepted canons of logic. The trend of the whole scriptural interpretation, with the Beast and Dragon of the *Book of Revelations* as a basis,—the astronomical, chronological and historical data are all marshalled up in serried array, to proclaim to an oppressed and yearning mankind, that the year in which spiritual and civil Tyranny was to have its deathknell sounded, was now (1795) dawning—"yea even at the door."

At the present time the whole production would be classed in the category of mild curiosities,—the lucubrations of a theologically stunted mind, like the acrostic arouse a sympathetic smile, and charitably be consigned to the wastebasket. Not so in an age when the minister was still the visible mouthpiece of Divine truth. No doubt the production would have remained unnoticed were it not for the extremely bitter and inflammable tone in which it was written. Its spirit would have done no mean credit to a Colton or Hooker,—a spirit which burned the Catholics at the stake, drove out the Quakers, sent Roger Williams to find an asylum among the Indians, and sat in judgment on the witches of Salem and Andover.

It was the incendiary character of the epitome, with its uncalled for aspersions on the Catholics of this country, who were just beginning to show signs of life and activity after the removal of the disabilities and proscription which so effectually hampered their careers, that inspired Bishop Carroll to whom the article was referred to issue the subjoined letter. The letter without entering into a categorical refutation of the whimsical ebullition, points out the undercurrent of bigotry and persecution which lies concealed in the whole document,—and which was liable to injure the cause of Catholicity and liberty. The letter is addressed

"TO THE EDITOR OF THE CARLISLE GAZETTE.*

"Living at a great distance I have seldom an opportunity of reading your paper, but I chanced this day to meet with that of Aug. 5th in which you communicate to the public your idea of a free press, and inform them of the rules by which you propose to conduct it. Every

---

* *Am. Cath. Hist. Researches*, Vol. xi, p. 133.

one who regards the peace of society must approve your determination, but should not your rules extend farther than to the protection of individuals? Should a public paper, supported by public patronage and destined for the purpose of political information become the vehicle of abuse against any religious society, living under the protection of our common constitution and laws? Should this Society, through the medium of the *Gazette* of Carlisle, be devoted to the execration of their fellow Christians? While with a praiseworthy spirit of Independence and philanthropy, you refuse to prostitute your press to the injury of a single individual : and should you not have refused to print in the same paper extracts from a work of the most rancorous fanaticism, the only purpose of which can be to raise up hostile hatred and violent animosities against a numerous body of Christians as dutiful to the laws and inoffensive to their fellow citizens as any in the United States. Who Bickeno was, or who the R. Rob. Davidson D.D. is, I know not ; but I want no other evidence than the extracts in your *Gazette*, to be convinced of the wild and ignorant fanaticism of the former. As to the Dr. of Divinity, I am tempted even on this serious subject to smile at *his* theological acquirements, who can submit to employ his leisure in epitomizing such a miserable production as Bickeno's, and give a new dress 'to the tale revived, the lie so oft o'erthrown.' I can hardly think him serious.

"But to return to yourself, Mr. Editor, after having disseminated seeds of violent hatred against Roman Catholics, as forming the very kingdom of antichrist; could you in justice refuse them the rights of defence, and even of retaliation against their adversaries if they insisted on it? If they were to offer for publication writings tending to prove that Luther and Calvin, and Henry the 8th, and Archbishop Cranmer, and John Knox began to spread the reign of antichrist, and that their followers support it until this day, and share their guilt; (and I assure you that this may be done with much better arguments than those of Duumvirs Bickno and his epitomizer) would you admit those writings as fit for insertion in your Gazette? In my opinion you would not; and whatever you might now resolve to do, after having sent forth the predictions of prophet Bickno and left yourself no fair plea for rejecting a free examination of them; I am persuaded, that you would have reprobated (?) and with great propriety, similar inflammatory pieces, on the Catholic side of the question. I expect however the insertion of this as a necessary animadversion on the author, or authors of those injurious extracts given in your paper; and shall estimate your fair dealing and impartiality by your readiness in complying with a reasonable and just request."

"Aug. 11, 1795."   [*Signed.*]   "CATHOLICUS."

The reply was never published. The motive that

prompted its suppression was more the fear of arousing animadversive consequences, than the plea of rejecting it on the score of inutility. Had the letter been written in the year 1895 instead of 1795, it could not be more opportune and apposite, nor reflect the wanton disregard of all fairness and decency—a century ago—not even as virulent as it has been of late, when the Catholic was the butt of the foulest and most venomous attacks, and when sheets literally reeking with filth and obscenity, were scattered broadcast throughout the country, and smuggled into the homes of pure women and innocent girls. This under the cloak of religion!

The editor of the *Gazette*, though not a most conscientious Christian, (for in searching the files of his journal, we detect advertisements calling attention to the printing office having on stock Tom Paine's "Age of Reason" side by side with the latest theological tract vindicating the "Divinity of Christ,") had not the courage to print the Bishop's letter, and had recourse to the following transparent evasion.*

"The Editor acknowledges the receipt of the piece signed Catholicus. He can assure the writer, that the extracts from a pamphlet entitled the 'Signs of the Times' were not intended to give any offence to any society of Christians whatever; but merely to inform such as might

---

* *Kline's Carlisle Weekly Gazette*, Sept. 12, 1795.

be curious to inquire into the prophetic parts of Scripture, what are the sentiments of some writers of the present day, respecting the fall of civil and religious tyranny in the Old World; and what aspect the revolutions that have lately happened may have towards that event. The Epitomizer made a few extracts for his own use; which being shown to some of his friends they desired they might be printed. As to his own sentiments of the work, how far it agrees with the most approved commentators, and in what parts it may be exceptionable, he has said nothing. He will neither support nor condemn it through the medium of a newspaper, having done nothing more than faithfully made a few extracts from a work which the public is already in possession of; as he would make extracts from any book whatever, which he might think curious and deserving attention,—as the piece is far from being in the style of argumentation, the Editor begs to be excused from publishing it.''

ROGER BROOKE TANEY.

At the same time that *The Signs of the Times* was luridly appearing on the religious horizon of Carlisle, probably a very interested party in the discussion was a Catholic young man who was pursuing his studies at Dickinson College and would graduate in a few weeks. The young student was descended from an old Catholic

Maryland stock, whose history was almost coincident with that of Lord Baltimore's arrival on these shores, and some of whose ancestors were not only gentlemen of means, but persons of literary culture, having made their studies in St. Omers and Bruges, both names familiar to the reader. As a young lad of fifteen years he was sent to Dickinson College in 1792. The reason Dickinson College was chosen in preference to any other, especially a Catholic institution, was primarily, because two young neighbors were attending it at the time, and secondarily its president, Dr. Nisbet, had almost international fame for varied and extensive learning. He gives us a circumstantial narrative of his adventurous trip from Baltimore to Carlisle, how an unfavorable wind kept the schooner, on which he embarked on the Patuxent River, laden with merchandise and produce, nearly a week from port. Since there was no stage between the two points, they had to wait until a wagon returning to Carlisle took them and their trunks. After trundling two weeks on the roads of which we can form but a faint conception, they arrived safely in Carlisle. Here he remained until 1795,—and during this time went home but twice on vacation, and on both occasions walking on foot, accomplishing the feat in two days. The estimated distance is eighty-five miles.

Whilst here he was a great favorite with Dr. Nisbet, in whose home he was an ever-welcome guest, and whose kindness he always recalled with emotion, affection and gratitude. His talents already displayed themselves in a manner not only to merit the praise of his teachers, the admiration of his classmates, but presaged a future that could not fail to be successful, if not brilliant.

He graduated on October 7, 1795, receiving the degree of Bachelor of Arts. Being elected by his fellow students as valedictorian on commencement day he addressed a vast concourse in the Presbyterian Church "with a brief account of the utility of Seminaries of learning."*

It is not our province to trace the unprecedented strides this young man made to success; how by a succession of brilliant achievements he rose to the most distinguished honors in the nation; what an important part he played in shaping its destinies; and how he attained the highest eminence barring that of President, and that in spite of factional animosities and political persecution and abolitionist execration the name of *Roger Brooke Taney* † will always remain one of the most honored in the history of American jurisprudence and patriotism. An honor to his country and to his Church.

His devotion to his Church was that of the most devout and uncompromising Catholic. "Most thankful am I, that the reading, reflection, studies and experience of a long life have strengthened and confirmed my faith in the

---

* *Carlisle Gazette.* Oct. 9, 1795.
† Born March 17, 1777.—Appointed Chief Justice, March 15, 1836. Died Oct. 12, 1864, aged 87 years.

Catholic Church, which has never ceased to teach her children how they should live and how they should die."*

His humility was as profound as his faith, and was exercised in even the most solemn as well as trivial circumstances of his life. "Often have I seen him stand at the outer door leading to the confessional, in a crowd of penitents, the majority *colored*, waiting his turn for admission. I proposed to introduce him by another door to my confessional, but he would not accept of any deviation from the established custom."†

At the time of young Taney's sojourn in Carlisle, Dickinson College was a small structure of four rooms, located in Liberty Alley,—immediately back of Bedford street, (in the rear of the present Cumberland Fire Co. Engine House,) and was consequently only a few hundred yards from the chapel. His attendance there whenever the presence of a priest gathered together the small congregation in the modest log chapel, is more than a matter of mere surmise, since in addition to his strong and vital faith, which was the inspiration of his holy life, he certainly must have had a personal acquaintance with some of the Maryland missionaries, who at this time visited Carlisle.

---

* *Memoir of Roger B. Taney. LL.D.*, p. 475.
† *Memoir of Roger B. Taney, LL.D.*, p. 476.

Death of Archbishop Carroll.

It was during the pastoral administration of Father De Barth that Archbishop John Carroll was called to his heavenly reward, Dec. 3, 1815. The sad news filled the hearts of the faithful with the most poignant grief,—and all Americans irrespective of political or church affiliation seemed to realize that in his death the Church had lost one of its most powerful champions and the Republic one of its most loyal sons. His zeal and sincerity both as an ecclesiastic and citizen seemed to have made his death one that all lamented,—for it was only now, that the full sense of loss dawned upon the mind of all lovers of virtue and liberty. Always foremost in the assertion and maintenance of the heritage of liberty handed down to us, he yet joined a childlike piety and an ascetic mode of life, that elicited the veneration of all who came in contact with him. That this influence did not confine itself to his immediate circle of acquaintances or local environment, is manifest from the eloquent and touching eulogy which appeared in the *Carlisle Volunteer*, (Dec. 19, 1815,) and which bears evidence of being written by a non-Catholic. It is a great pleasure to reproduce the obituary in its entirety, *viz.*:

"Died at Baltimore on the 3d inst. in the 80th year of his age, the right reverend Doctor John Carroll, Arch Bishop, of Baltimore.

"The closing solemnities with which the body of the late Arch-Bishop Carroll, was entombed on Tuesday, brought together a greater crowd than we have ever witnessed on a similar occasion. The great, and the rich, and the poor, and the lowly, assembled to pay the last tribute of respect to the memory of this good and illustrious prelate. The Chapel which has been so long cherished by his fostering care, was crowded at an early hour, and the multitude who assembled without, seemed rather to indicate that some great public ceremony was to be performed, than some national calamity to be deplored The corpse of the venerable Archbishop which had lain in state, since the preceding Sunday was now enclosed in the coffin, surmounted by his mitre and pastoral crozier, and surrounded by those emblems which unite the fancy with the heart in solemn devotion. After the celebration of High Mass, the procession moved through Saratoga and Franklin streets, to the Chapel of the Seminary; which was designated as the place of interment.—We have never witnessed a funeral procession, where so many of eminent respectability and standing among us, followed the train of mourners.—Distinctions of rank, of wealth, of religious opinion were laid aside, in the great testimony of respect to the memory of the man.—Besides the numerous crowd who filled the streets, the windows were thronged with spectators.—The funeral service for the dead was performed at the Chapel of the Seminary; and the mind already penetrated with regret and deepest sorrow, felt the effect of these religious ceremonies, which performed in the same manner, and chaunted in the same language and tone of voice through succeeding ages bring together the remotest periods of 1600 years, and present to the mind, some faint image of eternal duration.—The deep tones of the organ and the solemn chaunt of the choristers seemed to the excited feeling, not to belong to this world, but to be the welcome of good spirits, who had gone before, and now solemnly saluted him, who descended through the tomb to the bar of eternal justice, to receive the reward apportioned to a good and faithful servant.

"According to the particular disposition of every one, have we heard the venerable Arch-Bishop praised and lamented—the extent of this knowledge and the enlargement of his mind, fastened upon the men of liberal science. The liberality of his character and his christian charity endeared him to his Protestant brethren, with whom he dwelt in brotherly love. He was a patriot and loved his native land ; nor should Americans forget that his exertions and benedictions, as a man and as a christian prelate, were given to the cause and the independence of his country. His manners were mild, impressive, and urbane. The various stores of knowledge came from his lips with uncommon classical grace and richness, which he gained from a perfect acquaintance with ancient languages and literature. His charities were only bounded by his means, and they fell around him like the dews of Heaven, gentle and unseen. To those who stood not in need of the comforts of life, he administered the consolation of his counsel ; and the weight of his character and reputation for erudition and profound good sense, gave an authority to his advice, which the proudest scarcely dared to disregard. The veil of mourning that hid the tears of the afflicted, covered many a heart not of his own particular flock, which felt that it lost an inestimable friend. The character of Arch-Bishop Carroll seemed indeed to be filled up with wonderful care. Educated at St. Omer's, he was early disciplined in the exercises of the mind, and deeply versed in classic lore. Becoming at Liege attached to the Society of Jesus, he acquired that spirit of action,—that profound knowledge of the human heart,—that admirable fitness for the affairs of the world, which for 200 years distinguished their order and spread its power to the remotest countries. When the glories of the Jesuits were extinguished with the society itself, he travelled over

Europe as the friend and instructor of an English nobleman. Then he viewed the manners of different nations—saw the courts of kings, and meetings of philosophers, and added the liberality of a true philosopher and, the accomplishments of a gentleman, to the apostolic dignity of his calling.—Temptation drew forth the purity of his virtue and like Shadrach he walked erect in the flames. He early marked the rise of the baleful meteor of French Philosophy, and mourned when he saw the " pestilences shook from its horrid hair," invade his native land. But he gathered his spiritual children under his wings, and protected them in security; and he was permitted to live to see a different spirit prevail to witness a great revival of religion, and in the abundant prosperity of his particular church, to reap the harvest of his toil and labor of his life. When he was called to receive the reward of his many virtues, the excellence of his character shone out with fresher lustre, as he gradually set like the sun in mellowed splendor—Death, as if fearfully, attacked him with slow and cautious approaches. The paralysis, and consequent mortification of the lower extremities was complete, before his icy touch, ventured to chill the heart;—and even until the last moment, the noble faculties of the mind retained their pristine vigor. He enquired if a conveyance was prepared to take away his sister and weeping connections; told them the scene was about to close, and requested them to take rest and nourishment.

His countenance retained in death the benignant expression of life. His piety grew warmer as life closed, and the glow of religious hope was elevated almost to enthusiasm. 'Sir,' he said to an eminent Protestant divine, who observed that his hopes were now fixed on another world : 'Sir, my hopes have always been fixed on the cross of Christ.' Yet, humility tempered his confidence, and while a numerous circle surrounding his bed of death, were transported with veneration at the moral sublimity of his last moments, and his joyous expectations of a speedy release, he called to his friend and associate to read for him the 'Miserere mei Deus—Have mercy on me, O Lord'— Reversing the wish of Vespasian, he desired, were it practicable, to be placed on the floor, that he might expire in the posture of deepest humility, as a christian martyr, and an humble suppliant to an interceding Saviour. How do the boasted glories of philosophy fade before the death of such a man ! Socrates died with a cheerless and unknown futurity before him—Cato's indignant soul spurned the yoke of imperial Cæsar, and Seneca opened his veins and calmly discoursed of philosophy as life ebbed with the purple tide,—but it was not theirs to know the hope of the christian, which springs from a life of virtue and a pious soul, and which changes the tomb into the triumphal arch, through which the pilgrim passes into joyful eternity."

[*Signed.*]   "E."

CHAPTER VIII.

REV. PETER HELBRON, A PIONEER PRIEST OF WESTERN PENNSYLVANIA DIES ON HIS WAY HOME AT CARLISLE.—HIS ASTONISHING JOURNEYS IN THE DISCHARGE OF HIS DUTIES.—IN HIS WILL HE BEQUEATHES ALL HIS PROPERTY TO ST. PATRICK'S CONGREGATION. — PURCHASE OF THE BLAINE LOTS FOR A RECTORY BY THOMAS HAGAN.

It was during the pastorate of Father De Barth, that one of the old pioneer missionaries, while on his way to Philadelphia in search of medical aid breathed his last in the home of Thomas Hagan, in Carlisle.

But few biographical data are available concerning this man, but those few stamp him as a fit companion for men like a Gallitzin, Barth and Brosius. Discomfort and hardship, the restrictions of a language whose unfamiliarity narrowed his career and circumscribed his influence, not even the realization that he was affected with an acute disease, which he, not unskilled in the practise of medicine, knew fully well would cause his death,—deterred him from performing missionary work which even in the light of modern traveling facilities, would seem simply stupendous. The ready acquiescence and unruffled cheerfulness with which he accepted the most toilsome and obnoxious missions, with but one dominant thought in view—the Glory of God and the salvation of souls, reveals to us the priest according to the heart of God. His sojourn in any mission was too brief to affix to it the impress of his individuality, —but his unobtrusive and unsparing labors were none the less meritorious in the sight of heaven and salutary to the souls entrusted to his care.

The antecedents of Rev. Peter Helbron, before his arrival in America are involved in considerable mystery. No doubt of German extraction, he must have known of the dearth of priests in this country and volunteered to join the self exiled heroes, who were accomplishing such noble work. The first record we have of him is that "Rev. Petrus Hulbrun and the Rev. John Bapt. Hulbrun,[*] arrived in Pennsylvania on board the ship Dorothea, master, from Rotterdam, Oct. 14th, 1787." He was at once appointed to Goshenhoppen, Berks Co.—for in the will of the Rev. John Lewis,[†] made in April, 1788, Elkton Cecil Co., Md.—he bequeathes all his property to Rev. Robert Molyneux, including "all my estate in Hereford township, save that in the tenure of R. J. Baptist De Ritter, now of Rev. Peter Helbron, Berks county."

On Aug. 19th, 1791, we find him installed as the second pastor of the church of the Holy Trinity, Philadelphia, where he succeeded his brother John Charles, who returned

---

[*] *Penna. Archives*, (II Series,) Vol. XVII, p. 532.
[†] *Records of the Am. Cath. Hist. Soc.*, Vol. I, p. 158.

to Europe in 1791. He was of course elected to the position by the Trustees of the church,—but since Bishop Carroll cheerfully gave his approbation to the selection, the impending storm which proved so harmful to the prestige, and mischievous to the development of Catholicity, was temporarily checked. The Philadelphia recollections represent him as a man of culture and refinement ; punctiliously neat and precise in his priestly attire and duties ; with a dignified and commanding presence ; sitting his horse with a military grace and repose that formed an unfailing source of admiration to his flock, and perhaps was not untinctured with a little pardonable vanity on the part of the rider. This accomplishment, which tradition recalls in the Alleghanies as well as Philadelphia, is easily accounted for by the fact that Father Helbron had done military duty in Prussia before his elevation to the priesthood.

The scandalous and disastrous conflict of the Trustees of Trinity Church with ecclesiastical authority began on Nov. 16th, 1796, when in defiance of episcopal authority and in flagitious violation of its own laws, the Trustees elected Rev. John Nepomucen Goetz as its pastor. This contumacious act, not only displaced Father Helbron, caused Bishop Carroll an endless amount of mortification and sorrow, disrupted the precarious unity, then the only hope of Catholic success, but laid the seeds for that calamitous epoch—the Hoganite schism. The congregation was divided into two embittered factions,—for the encounter was more than a mere ecclesiastical passage at arms. Father Helbron with the loyal Catholics retired to St. Joseph's Church;—Goetz, the Trustees and seceders took possession of Trinity Church. Goetz, though formally excommunicated, was still upheld and supported by the Trustees. This melancholy condition of affairs existed until 1802 when Father Elling and the Trustees made their submission to the Bishop of Baltimore. During these three years Father Helbron was at St. Joseph's until the fall of 1799 when he was appointed pastor of Sportsman's Hall, Westmoreland County, the present large Benedictine Abbey, St. Vincent's, and mother house of the order in America. He took possession on November 17th. The scandalous misconduct of his predecessor here also had not only spiritually played havoc with faith, but criminally alienated the church property, which only after wearisome and expensive litigation came into rightful possession again. After spending the holidays with his little congregation, saying mass in a stuffy little room of his log house, he returned to Philadelphia for a brief visit. The following entry in the mutilated church records of Carlisle, in Father Helbron's own hand, written in German, gives evidence of the methodical exactness for which he was always conspicuous. "On the 14th day of May, 1800, R. Petrus Helbron returned to his place sportsmanhal, in Westmoreland."

From this we can date the beginning of his career on the other side of the Alleghanies. Familiarized with his new charge he at once set about to build a home for himself,—a log house 28 × 26 feet, to which the congregation, now thoroughly enthusiastic did the best it could, by attaching a rude shed to the house, to answer as a chapel, until favorable circumstances would permit the erection of a more worthy habitation for our Lord. There was a superfluous abundance of wood, nor were joyous hearts and willing hands wanting to hasten the completion of this primitive temple,—but there was a deterrent absence of ——nails. They were an expensive commodity in those days, doubly so in the wild and primeval Alleghanies. But this did not balk the enthusiasim of our fervid Catholics. One of their number, Henry Kuhn, took his horse and saddle-bags, and came east over the mountains to raise sufficient funds to purchase nails. No doubt could the old list of contributors be discovered, more than one Carlisle name would be found on it,—for Carlisle was then the commerical emporium west of Philadelphia and Lancaster, and actually had a brick Catholic Church—a marvel in those days.

In 1810, the first church proper was built. A log structure of course, with the cathedral—like proportions of 40 × 27 feet. It had the luxury of a pine floor, but still remained unplastered.

From Sportsman's Hall Father Helbron made those

astonishing and lengthy excursions which would seem to us improbable, if not impossible, did we not know that he was an expert horseman, and did not his military nicety of detail, record every visit. In October, 1803—he visited "all stations beyond the Alleghany and Monongahela. On Oct. 22nd, he was in Buffalo N. Y. and records no less than thirty-eight baptisms in one day. In September, 1805, he again visited Buffalo and forty-one baptisms find an entry in the Registers, for the 26th, 28th, and 30th of that month. April 26th, 1812 we again find him there baptizing fifteen persons on the same day."

In the same year (1805) "he visited *five* counties baptizing ninety children, and even then, writing from Pittsburg, he said he would visit Washington, Roundstone, and York River before he returned home."[*]

During all this time Dr. Helbron, as he was familiarly called was on the most intimate and brotherly terms with Father Gallitzin, his neighbor. Their mutual interchange of visits was frequent, and at times prolonged into days and weeks. We can readily imagine the intercourse of these holy souls, their minds fired with zeal, their hearts aglow with love of God and man, their every action a mute but prayerful adoration of the Providence of God, which had sent them into these uninhabitable surround-

---

[*] Shea, *Life of Archbishop Carroll*, p. 451.

ings as embassadors of His Word and dispensers of His mysteries. Like the Fathers of the Desert, who only broke their perpetual silence, when issuing from their solitude to pay occasional visits to each other, the moments of which were consecrated to the discourse of holy things, animating each other with intensified ardor, so these patriarchs of our holy Faith sought each other to find solace in their tribulation, counsel in their perplexities, mutual inspiration in their discouragements. This was done not so much as an incentive for mental diversion, as to extend the scope of their usefulness, increase the ardor of their zeal, and promote the glory of God. Such visits could only accentuate their holy mission, and redouble their efforts to reclaim and preserve the widely scattered flock of Christ entrusted to their care.

His advanced age, debilitated body, and above all the fatal malady—a tumor on his neck, which once before baffled the surgeon's knife, were now giving unmistakable indications that he could not enjoy a much more extended lease of life. He never received, nor for that matter accepted or expected a salary, but supported his frugal wants from a small patrimony attached to the parish, and the profits accruing from its farm. His patrimony had undergone an ominous shrinkage, his experiments as a farmer were destined to lamentable failure,—the malignant tumor was threatening a fatal issue. In this dire extremity, his congregation raised a handsome subscription for him to go east and seek more capable medical skill since local physicians could do nothing for him. He left for Philadelphia—a journey of 280 miles to consult some specialist. The operation was performed—but was soon followed by fatal results, of which no doubt he had premonitory symptoms. His heart yearned for his old mountain home, for his abandoned and expectant flock,—and the effort to spend his declining days in their midst was gallantly made. Divine Providence, however, shaped matters differently.

On his return trip his condition became so alarming that he could not proceed further than Carlisle. Here, no doubt, he had formed some acquaintance during his former visits to Philadelphia. He found a warm welcome and an affectionate care in the home of Thomas Hagan and his wife Mary. Their home was then on East High (now Main) Street, where the Henderson block now is. Here they kept a store. His sickness was of brief duration, and he died here, April 24th, 1816.

In his dying moments, he made a will in which he bequeathed all his estate real and personal to Mary Hagan in trust for the Catholic Congregation at Carlisle. Why this was done to the exclusion of Sportsman's Hall remains inexplicable. The following is the will.*

---

* Recorded in *Will Book H.*, p. 390.

"I, Peter Helbrune being of sound and disposing mind and memory, blessed be got for the same, and being duly sensible of the short continuance of this mortal life do make this my last will and testament in manner and form following to wit: I give and device all my estate real and personal unto Mary Hagan, wife of Thomas Hagan to hold to her heirs and assigns (in trust) for the use of the Catholic Church in the Borough (*of Carlisle*)* for ever after first deducting all expenses that she may be at in attending me in my last illness and the expenses of my funeral: the money owing me from my estate to be applied to the said Church in such a way as the trustees of said Church shall think proper, and do hereby nominate constitute and appoint Thomas Hagan of the borough of Carlisle to be sole executor of this my last said will and testament.

"Interlineations made before signing

"Signed sealed and proclaimed to be the said will and testament of Peter Helbron, this day of 22nd April 1816 in the presence of
  John A. Black,
  W. Ramsey"

[Signed]. "PETER + HELBRONE"
His Mark

---

* Words in Italics were interlined.

He was buried in the immediate rear of the old church, and when the annex was built in 1823, it covered both it and other graves which surrounded it. No tombstone marked his last resting place, and the spot that contained his remains, was left undisturbed when the present church was built in 1893. The spot is immediately opposite the statue of St. Patrick, under the communion railing.

Though a man of scrupulous nicety and punctilious method in the discharge of his priestly duties, the result of thorough ecclesiastical training, as much as an outgrowth of his military career, in financial affairs, as well as farming he displayed an inaptitude and simplicity that would be droll, were in not that it caused him much anxiety in life, and resulted in litigation after his death. He seemed to lack all powers of adaptability to conform to the customs and language of his adopted country. European methods, especially those in vogue in thrifty and frugal Germany, were utterly impracticable in this country with its unbroken forests and virgin soil. His ignorance of the English language, which he took little or no pains to acquire, lead him to many misunderstandings, and involved him in unpleasant collisions with those with whom he had commercial transactions. A giant in the service of God— he was a child in the business activities of life. This was especially conspicuous in the singular, not to say eccentric manner in which he managed his farm. An inventory of his estate at the time of his death shows that he had no less than five horses, seven head of cattle, besides a large number of sheep, hogs and calves. All told, he had thirty animals that not only needed feed and stabling and care in winter, but which even under the most favorable circumstances would be a drain on his cash account, not to allude to the inadequate, even expensive shifts he was reduced to keep them alive. The consequence was, that frequent and protracted absences from home obliged him to trust to the capacity and integrity of others, which in the one case was misplaced, and in the other repeatedly abused, and naturally debts were incurred which he could not pay.

An inventory of his estate reveals the fact that it was appraised at $1414.19, of this he carried $104.11 on his person at the time of his death. Claims came from all directions, as they invariably do in such cases. One on a note endorsed by Gen. James O'Hara, of Pittsburg, amounted to $311.82. The balance found by the Orphans Court for distribution amounted to but $325.58½. This was handed to the executor Thomas Hagan. What disposition was made of this balance cannot be ascertained, although the writer recalls reading somewhere that Father Dwen in a letter to Bishop Conwell claimed that it was appropriated as the testator directed. Of this there can be no doubt, since both Hagan and his wife were persons of sturdy honesty, and most zealous Catholics besides.

The final disposition of the legacy, can perhaps be accounted for by a purchase Thomas Hagan made, a year after Father Helbron's death, by which the lot and stone house adjoining the church was acquired, and which is now occupied by the Rectory. On April 16, 1817,* he purchased from Ephraim Blaine, the grandfather of the Hon. James G. Blaine, a lot 60 ft. front and 260 ft. in length, with a stone house on it, for the sum of $800.00. Ephraim Blaine was Commissary General in the Revolutionary army, and a man of means and influence. The object in view, in making this purchase was obviously to hold it for the church until such a time when it could be purchased. The whole transaction reflects great credit on the sagacity and foresight of Mr. Hagan. He held it until 1820, when on May 20th,† he and his wife transferred it to the Rev. Francis O'Neill " Treasurer of the Jesuit Society and to his successors in office in trust for the use of the Roman Catholic Congregation in the Borough of Carlisle." The consideration was the same as that of the first purchase $800.

From this it would seem that Mr. Hagan employed the $325.00, balance of Father Helbron's legacy, in this purchase, the balance being raised either by the congregation, or the munificence of the Conewago Jesuits. The house was an old stone affair, with a large vegetable garden attached, which was usually rented and the proceeds devoted to assist in paying the pastor his nameless salary.

---

* Recorded in *Deed Book DD*, p. 23. Dated April 7, 1817.

† Recorded in *Deed Book EE*, Vol. I, p. 550. Dated May 20, 1820.

CHAPTER IX.

REV. GEORGE D. HOGAN, FIRST RESIDENT PASTOR.—THE EXPOSURE OF REV. WILLIAM HOGAN, THE SCHISMATIC.—INTERESTING CORRESPONDENCE BETWEEN FATHER HOGAN AND BISHOP CONWELL.—ISAAC BROWN PARKER, ESQ., SENDS ON AN AFFIDAVIT.—FATHER HOGAN AND CHIEF JUSTICE GIBSON.

The increasing Catholic population, the formation of new settlements, the dearth of priests and the growing infirmities of those engaged in the vast and laborious field, made it paramount to see that capable, efficient and zealous men would come forward to step into the depleted ranks. The dire need of priests, both German and English-speaking, grew daily more apparent, and only became more accentuated in view of the stream of immigration pouring its thousands on our shores. Appeals were made to Ireland and Germany, and were responded to most readily by a self-sacrificing body of men, who were fully impressed with the magnitude of the task that confronted them, but had barely an idea of the hardships and privations that would have to be endured. The consequence was that many a brave heart sank and fiery zeal dampened—when the extreme poverty, the small numerical strength, the vast distances separating the missions, the heterogeneous nationalities constituting the parishes, the repellant attitude of sectarian bigotry—were viewed for the first time face to face—and the abstract idea became a stunning reality. The Jesuits, inured to a life of deprivation and poverty—bore the ordeal heroically, even cheerfully—but many of the secular priests unconsciously recoiled from a work, which they had not unreasonably concluded would shorten their lives and perhaps be productive of little appreciable good in the end.

Unfortunately the New World had already become an asylum not only for the oppressed, but for many who had the choice between solitary confinement in some reformatory institution, or precipitate flight to America, of becoming a burden to society in some workhouse or eleemosynary asylum, or searching for pastures new in this country of the broadest liberty. Many availed themselves of the latter alternative. Among the ecclesiastical recusants who came to the new country there were found priests who at times had been questionable ornaments of their profession, and who, having exhausted the patience of their spiritual superiors and being at the end of their canonical tethers, sought this new country, not so much for rehabilitating their smirched character or atoning for their flagrant conduct as to have a new license and a more inviting field to ply their avocation of scandal, greed, shame, and disgrace. This, to the incalculable detriment of religion, the irreparable scandal to non-Catholics and the irremediable ruin of souls. America became not only the dumping ground of undesirable immigrants, but the refuge of disaffected and recalcitrant priests. One of these, and probably the most mischievous and abandoned that America had as yet seen, whose malign influence retarded the work of the Church in Pennsylvania, for more than twenty years, at a stage of her existence when a lasting schism seemed both imminent and possible, was a man whose name is alway inseparably connected with that of the first resident pastor, (resident pastor in a measure, as we shall see) of Carlisle.

A new era begins in the history of St. Patrick's Congregation with the advent of the Rev. George Denis Hogan, who was literally its first resident pastor, usually dividing his time between York and Carlisle, with Conewago as headquarters, if the term may be used, for the want of a better.

Formerly the missionaries from Conewago attended all the churches that were attached to it, by a precedent sanctioned by custom or ecclesiastical authority, we are unable to state. Now they seem to have been apportioned off, and allotted to the pastoral care of duly appointed priests. The method had much to commend in it. It relieved the priest of fatiguing journeys, brought him more in touch with his congregation, to study, feel and relieve their necessities, attend to their spiritual wants, and permitted a more concentrated effort in working for the material prosperity of both church and people.

Rev. G. D. Hogan was born in Limerick, Ireland, and came from a stock that gave the church a number of (some of them prominent) priests. Whether he was invited by V. Rev. de Barth, who was then administrator of the diocese of Philadelphia, could not be ascertained. It was the latter, however, who sent him to St. Mary's Seminary, Baltimore, in 1819 to prepare for ordination. He had made his studies in Maynooth College, received minor orders there, a sufficient warrant that he was a man of intellectual parts, if not ripe scholarship. His studies at St. Mary's were brief, consisting of nothing more than an immediate preparation for the holy priesthood. He entered the Seminary, December 29th, 1819—received subdeaconship and deaconship March 20th and 21st, 1820, at the hands of Archbishop Maréchal in St. Peter's Church, Baltimore, and was raised to the holy priesthood by the same prelate on the 25th of the same month, in the chapel of the Seminary. In October (15th, 1821) he was appointed to serve Carlisle and York conjointly, as pastor.

His career here was too brief to permit a proper estimate being made of his character or ability. A scholarly man, he must have been, the endorsement of Maynooth places him on this score,—beyond the range of a doubt or peradventure. The church records prove him to have been methodical, precise and neat in the performance of his parochial work. The literary remains that have been handed down to us bear the stamp of a well disciplined mind, a ready and copious command of unimpeachable English and a sturdy faith. Of a vacillating temperament, disappointed in the prospects held out, physically unable to perform the arduous work of the mission, and above all the impending ecclesiastical cataclysm eventually caused by his namesake of unsavory reputation and inglorious memory, made him yearn to return to his old home. Upon repeated application he received his dismissory letter (*exeat*) to return to his native land. This he did in July, 1822,* serving less than two years on the American missions.

In Carlisle he is mainly recalled by the incidents of his arrest by one of his parishioners for an unpaid boarding bill—which is narrated more circumstantially later;—and by the fact that he usually spent two weeks at Carlisle and York alternately, thus becoming more intimately acquainted with his parishioners, and leaving a proportionately better impression on their lives and faith.

He however entered into historic prominence by his exposé of the life and habits of his cousin, Rev. William Hogan, whose malodorous reputation, scandalous career and calamitous rebellion, caused the first and most disastrous schism the Church ever experienced in this country.

Rev. William Hogan was a priest of "shady" antecedents before he came to this country,—and no doubt his

---

* According to Bishop Newman's *Diary*, he died in Paris the same year; " *Paris 1822.*"

conduct and history was such that he considered his career virtually at an end, as far as Ireland was concerned. On his arrival here, he received faculties to exercise priestly functions in Albany, and to be near his kinsman, sought admission to the Philadelphia diocese. Not having proper letters of dismissal (*exeat*) he was admitted conditionally by Father De Barth, the administrator. About the same time Bishop Conwell was consecrated bishop, and took possession of his new see December 2, 1820.

The conduct of Rev. William Hogan was such as to demand ecclesiastical censure, which was not only resented by him, but called forth a perfect tempest of indignation on the part of the parishioners, fanned by the incendiary harangues of the temporary pastor of St. Mary's, which he claimed to possess by canonical right. The whole affair is discussed more fully in the next chapter,— but it is broached here to introduce some letters exchanged between the litigant parties, in which Father George Hogan, while pastor of Carlisle, did yeoman work in the cause of truth, and unveiled the masquerading hypocrisy and perjured villainy of his cousin, in a manner that should have proved fatal to all his pretensions. Eventually they set the seal of falsehood, and branded as a blasphemous apostate a man who like all of his stripe, run their meteoric course in the briefest space of time. In leaving the Church, the anticipated secession of Catholics of course failed to take place; in marrying consecutively two widows, he took God's punishments into his own hands, and in dying a death of despair, he but followed the footsteps of his precursor in the Apostolic college, whose memory is held up to eternal execration.

Bishop Conwell was not the most approachable of men. His assumption of prerogatives, not entirely of an ecclesiastical nature, readily and reverently accorded in Catholic countries, was looked upon somewhat askance in this democratic atmosphere of liberty and equality. His reserve and coldness and unsympathetic demeanor, more than the exercise of arbitrary or dictatorial authority, chilled if it did not alienate the affections of some of his priests. At a time when Catholicity was in its mere formative state, a punctilious observance of all the straitlaced proprieties could easily have been dispensed with, and the exercise of the amenities of a more fraternal nature, been most advantageously cultivated. However this was more the result of trans-Atlantic training, than a desire to be assertive of his dignity or authority.

In the following letter, written whilst pastor at Carlisle, as in fact all the following letters were, Father G. Hogan takes the initiative in making a series of disclosures, that speedily and summarily brush away all of William Hogan's pretensions to piety and learning, and would have sounded the death knell of his shortlived popularity, had not the obstinacy of the church Trustees, under the glamor and thrall of the perverted priest, been blinded to all sense of christian duty. From all that can be learned of the Trustees and William Hogan, they must have formed an ideal admiration society. Never was there a body in which the chief received a more effusive and perpetual flattery, and repaid it by a more obsequious and elaborate condescension.

The correspondence, while it unravels a part of church history not commonly known,—gives a most comprehensive reflex of the arrogant priest and disgruntled Trustees. It reveals William Hogan to us, as a man whose love of flattery, inordinate vanity and overweening ambition not only unfitted him for missionary work, but already showed the unmistakable symptoms of rebellion and apostasy. The letters passed between Bishop Conwell, Father George, and William Hogan, will unfold the whole deplorable tale and its lamentable consequences. It will be noticed that those of Father George Hogan are not only written in a graceful English,—but breathe a warm piety and fervent faith.

The first is addressed :—

"TO THE RIGHT REV. THE BISHOP OF PHILADELPHIA.

"CONEWAGO, 20th of January, 1821.

"MY LORD :—

"If mutual confidence had been established between us, while I was in Philadelphia, I am inclined to believe that certain matters I intended to communicate, would lead to some beneficial consequences. But after much anxious reflection and consultation, I feel it still my painful duty to advise with your lordship concerning the line of conduct I am to pursue relative to Mr. Hogan. Your lordship may recollect that I mentioned to you, I perceived last summer, certain indications in him of exceptionable conduct as a clergyman. But my suspicions have been fully realized, when last in Philadelphia, by an explicit avowal of his sentiments. Without entering into a further detail for *the present*, they are such as entitle me to pronounce him unworthy of confidene as a Catholic priest. Of these facts, however, I believe I am the sole depository. Consequently they can be brought to bear upon your lordship's proceedings only as *ex post facto* proofs against him. It remains now to be determined by your lordship, whether at all, or in what manner, a disclosure on my part would serve the cause of religion. We have lived for years on terms of the strictest intimacy. His friends are aware that I am now in the same house with Mr. Debarth, whose hasty proceedings I before censured with some asperity. Appearing in these circumstances against Mr. H., they will reproach me with ingratitude, with inconsistency, perhaps also with interested views. Such obloquy, however, I disregard, only inasmuch as it may seem to give some colour to their calumny, and render my depositions fruitless. But if your lordship be of a contrary opinion, the only question that remains, is, in what manner am I to proceed? If I direct a public letter to Philadelphia, I will be deprived of the opportunity and advantage of a timely reply, which probably may be requisite. Besides, I will be stigmatized as a mere tool, worked upon by Mr. D. B. If I were to threaten Mr. H. with my intentions, this intimation may enable him before the public to defeat the success of my endeavors. Now, my lord, it strikes me, that if I were to be confronted with two or three of his leading friends, and that we be sworn to secrecy, my depositions would prevail with them either to abandon him, or be guided by prudent measures; but if your lordship views the matter in some other light, I am prepared to resign my conduct relative to this melancholy business, totally to your direction. I feel I am placed in a very trying predicament, otherwise I would not presume to obtrude any of the above suggestions upon your lordship's consideration. It requires very little research to foresee the jealousies and angry feelings my conduct is likely to occasion in our families at home, whilst the unthinking and malicious in the old and new world, will show me little mercy. But I confidently hope that the Lord whom I fear, will assist and protect me. I still entertain friendly and charitable feelings towards Mr. H. But my solemn duty to God, will always predominate over private considerations. I have now only to add, that if your lordship pleases, you may (under the veil of strict secrecy) show this letter to Mr. Cummisky

You have now only to speak, and rely on the ready compliance of your lordship's submissive subject,

 [*Signed.*]   "G. D. HOGAN,
"Near Abbottstown, Adams County, Pennsylvania."

"P. S.—Perhaps it may be necessary to mention, that Mr. Deborth is not at all concerned in this business."

The following is an answer to the above letter, by the Right Rev. Bishop Connell, which many conjectured might have held out an inducement to the Rev. G. D. Hogan, to make a subsequent disclosure.

      " PHILADELPHIA, January 27, 1821.
" REV. DEAR SIR,

"Yours of the 20th only came to hand this day. Your immediate compliance with my desire that you should return to Conewago, confirmed the good opinion I had of you before I saw you ; for I was previously led to believe by the relation of others, that you were under the influence of conscience, and had the fear of God in your heart, and nothing accordingly could induce me to signify the wish I had, that you should go back so suddenly, except the circumstances which you knew the clergy to be in here, for otherwise, I was disposed to retain you for a while at least, after conferring and consulting with the Rev. Mr. Barth. Considering that you were ordained for the diocese of Philadelphia, and entertaining the above opinion, I thought it by no means advisable to part with you, when state of religion required many more priests than are employed on the mission here at present, and therefore knowing as you do this to be the case, you cannot consider me as dealing unfairly with you, when I refused to give you an *exeat*, which probably on a reconsideration of the matter, you might be sorry for hereafter, if I had granted your request.

"The Rev. Mr. Hannan tells me, that if he had come sooner, he could have prevented the publication of the pamphlet, which Doctor Kelly thought he could have done, by threatening to divulge something he knew about him. If I knew the worst things possible of the gentleman in question, it would ill become me to give them publicity to the injury of the clerical order. I did not think proper to let Mr. Cummisky know anything of your communicaation; whatever intelligence I got of what came to your knowledge, I should be sorry to reveal or act upon as long as you wish it. Send me the particulars, and let me know how you and Mr. —— stand. Write to me by return of post.

"I am with affectionate regard,
    "Yours sincerely,
[*Signed.*] "HENRY, Bishop of Philadelphia."

In answer to the above the disclosure of Hogan's intended apostacy and the motives that lead to it are first broached, in a letter to Bishop Conwell, which reads as follows:

"CONEWAGO, 2d February, 1821.

"MY LORD,

"I feel unaffectedly grateful to your lordship for condescending to honour me with your complimentary and friendly letter, and connecting your authority with its divine source, shall always feel it my sacred duty to endeavour to meet your lordship's approbation. Though your lordship has charitably overlooked my indiscreet behaviour in Philadelphia, it is no less imperative on me to make what atonement lies in my power. I approached Philadelphia with a heavy heart from various causes; whilst subsequent apprehension, (perhaps unwarrantably indulged) aggravated my feelings and dictated certain irritable language, for which I now in the most unqualified manner solicit your lordship's indulgent forgiveness. After this digression prescribed by duty, I shall now cheerfully comply with your lordship's wishes in the following communication:

"Thinking me unwilling to go to Philadelphia, Mr. Hogan wrote to me, to meet him in Lancaster, which I accordingly did. Aware that I was under the impression of bad treatment, he imagined that a fair opportunity offered of warping my religious principles; with this view he very artfully proposed to me 'to accompany him to Bishop Hobart of New York, who would very eagerly receive us into his service, and that in a few years we might be able to lay by a comfortable provision for life." At the very mention of such a diabolical proposal, I got quite confounded, which of course interrupted the conversation. But after some interval, he again urged it with the most crafty ingenuity. I only answered him by insisting to hear no more about it; he then asked me 'if he went to Hobart would I then visit him;' I replied not; he then inquired 'would I speak to him,' to which I replied, I might if I met him accidentally. He then observed, 'I was like all young priests, pious for the first two years, but that he never met one, who retained any faith, and that he never knew an honest man among them but one,' mentioning his name, who by the bye was as vapid a fox as himself. This antichristian calumny of course I reprobated in his presence. All this I intended to communicate to your lordship when I arrived in Philadelphia; on our way he remarked, that he wanted sadly to procure Luther's works. Though I had very little doubts of what he was upon, particularly after reading only a few pages of his pamphlet, yet to be fully satisfied, I asked him, did he since his suspension say regularly his office: to which he replied not, even for some time before, and that he never would. In the stage, some Protestants from Carlisle, male as well as female, traveled with us, who frequently heard me expatiate on the sanctified life of our clergy in general. But his conduct in their presence was so gross, and so disedifying, that I was frequently obliged to hang down my head in confusion. When your lordship refused to speak to me in private, I imagined then it was for want of confidence, which naturally mortified me sorely; I came back to him and asked would he accompany me to Ireland, if I obtained my *exeat*, he replied he would. This I did with a view to prevent him from apostasy; considering that if he went there, the persuasion of friends and remorse, might convert him. I however assured him, unless he disavowed all notions of apostasy, I would abandon him, and lie on my own oars: he then said he was not serious, in alluding to the apostasy alone, but in some time after declared 'he would not officiate as priest, he said he would (knowing me not to have passage money) bear my expenses to any diocese in the world, I chose to go to.' I have stated matters in order and even verbally as they occurred, that your lordship may judge whether I was warranted in deeming him unworthy of confidence as a Catholic priest any longer, or is there any reliance to be placed on his declaration in the circumstances I mention, that he was not serious. For my part, I solemnly declare, that I think it was expressed solely with the design to moderate my evident horror of the act, and I would be qualified to depose that I believe he is not tinctured with one remaining ray of Catholic faith. I differ in opinion in this, as well as in many other things, with Mr. Hannan, that he could prevent the publication of the pamphlet, had he arrived in due time. I am firmly persuaded (still I may be in error) that it was designed as a desperate resource of conscious guilt in this country. I feel sincerely indebted to your lordship, for your kind inquiry about my situation here. Whatever may be the occasional causes of my discontent, it is my sincere desire they shall not interfere with your lordship's arrangements. I am content to languish in passive silence here for many reasons, until your lordship can conveniently relieve me. In the dispensations of a benign Providence, it is meet I should suffer something for some imperfections from which I by no means claim an exemption ; I am resolved not to differ with Mr. D. B. upon any provocation. His former kindness to me, and correct conduct up to a venerable old age, ought to suppress every rising emotion caused only by his natural warmth of temper. But if your lordship do still desire it, I authorize the Rev. Mr. Cummiskey to show you a confidential letter I sent him yesterday, which is a faithful exposé of our misunderstandings here. I only received your lordship's letter this evening. I am preparing to start for Carlisle in the morning, which may account for the inaccuracies and omissions that are visible in this scrawl. I have not leisure to write it over, but will trust to your lordship's indulgence. I have the honour to be your lordship's obedient, obliged subject,

 [*Signed.*]   "G. D. HOGAN.
"Right Rev. Dr. Conwell."

There can be little question that the work of the missionary territory allotted to Father Hogan was exasperatingly extensive, and the primitive mode of travel too irksome to warrant his continuing in this field, unless it would prove highly detrimental to his health and thus impair his future usefulness, if not check his career entirely. By confining his work to the Carlisle and York parishes alone, to the exclusion of the smaller missions, physical recuperation on his part would go hand in hand with the spiritual advancement of the two parishes, and, therefore, he sent the following appeal to his Bishop:

"Conewago, 20th February, 1821.

"Content to submit to some occasional mortifications here, rather than perplex your lordship in the administration of your diocese, is the best proof I can give that I am not actuated by a vexatious spirit. Since I was ordained, I have attended these congregations nearly thirty miles asunder without a murmur. I now find, that consistent with my health I am no longer equal to its pressure, and therefore beg of your lordship in the most respectful urgent manner, to exempt me from attending Little York in future. I am perfectly satisfied to attend Carlisle twice a month. By remaining in Carlisle from Saturday until Monday week, the ride will not distress me, besides I will have an opportunity of forming them to habits of piety in the interim, which could scarce be expected, if I were only to be among them as before, two or three days a visit.

"Last week I received the following note from Mr. H.:"

"PHILADELPHIA, February 11th, 1821.

"My Dear George,

"Doctor Conwell is handing about a letter from you, in which you mention (as he expressed it,) that I intended to join Bishop Hobart. I don't believe you have written such a letter, as it would be false, or you misunderstood me. Perhaps I might have said, that my persecutions might almost drive any man to desperation. Write to me by return of post, a letter which I can show the public, saying that I only said that my persecutions would drive any man to desperation. I thought you were the last to injure me. You know well if I wished to join Hobart, or any other Protestant bishop, I might have done it long since, but I shall not sacrifice my faith nor my *honour.* Are you too, one of my persecutors? Let me know your answer by return of post, and let it be what it ought to be.

[*Signed.*] "WILLIAM HOGAN."

"After due deliberation, I answered him in the following manner:

"'I only received yesterday, your strange call upon me to retract what I mentioned to Dr. Conwell about you. I merely stated what literally occurred between us in Lancaster and afterwards, to justify me in believing you were *no longer* impressed with the principles and sentiments of a Catholic priest. If I be mistaken, no event ever occurred that will afford me greater satisfaction, neither will I have any hesitation in retracting (only as to his future conduct) my opinion even before the public, *should this be made certain*, until then '*quod scripsi scripsi.*' It appears one of your friends has mentioned that he could prevent the publication of your pamphlet, had he arrived in due time, by threatening to disclose some of your misconduct in Ireland. This I denied in my letter to Dr. C. as far as I knew, neither need you be afraid that I will ever reveal what passed between us in the moment of unreserved confidence, (nothing regarding his character). In writing that letter, my object was to reform you, and no matter who may blame me, I shall always feel the consolation of discharging a conscientious duty, both as a Christian and a friend. With the most sincere sympathy for your present unhappy situation, I am,' &c., &c.

"Before I sent off the letter, I consulted a discreet friend, and kept a copy, lest he might take an unfair advantage of the words I used. Your lordship can easily perceive my motive in replying at all, and in the manner: probably if I had seen his second pamphlet I would not notice his letter, which is the last I shall ever acknowledge, unless a sincere conversion ensues. But (alas!) this I never expect, unless the Lord interposes in a very extraordinary manner. In the infinitude of his charity, may he avert the consequences to religion, which shall be the fervent prayer of your lordship's obedient subject,

[*Signed.*] "G. D. HOGAN."

"Personally appeared before me, one of the aldermen for the city of Philadelphia, G. D. Hogan, who, on his solemn oath doth declare and say, that each of three letters signed G. D. Hogan, are his production, and that the facts therein are substantially correct.

[*Signed.*]   "G. D. HOGAN."

"Sworn and subscribed before me, this 24th day of February, 1821.

[*Signed:*]   "JOHN DOUGLASS, *Alderman.*"

Notwithstanding the above proofs of the Rev. Wm. Hogan's religious prevarications, a ludicrous attempt had been made by some of his friends to establish an inconsistency in the Rev. G. D. Hogan's conduct, by advancing some private confidential letters; in consequence of which, the following note was addressed to J. A. Esq. :

"PHILADELPHIA, 26th February, 1821.
"SIR,

"I never complained of your showing my private letters to your friends; but I did complain that you showed some of them, and suppressed the others, which established the purity of my motives, relative to the unfortunate individual whom you confessed to me you would abandon, if it were not for his present unhappy situation, and who, in *retort*, reproached his principal adherents as 'a parcel of rascals, employing him as tool to accomplish their own end.' The unhappy man was the cause of the bad treatment with which I acquainted you, and which (by glossing over dates and subsequent occurrences) you have endeavoured to pervert to the abhorrence of

[*Signed.*] "G. D. HOGAN."
"J. A. Esq."

"LANCASTER, 28th February, 1821.

"About five years ago, the Rev. William Hogan, now in Philadelphia, was suspended by Doctor Tuohy, R. C. Bishop of Limerick. In a few days after, he wrote a note to Dr. Warburton, the Episcopalian Bishop of Limerick, acquainting him that he wanted to see him upon *particular business.* Before he sent him this note, I happened to see it, and asked him for what purpose he wanted to see Doctor W. He replied he intended to become a Protestant clergyman, and that he called in person before upon Doctor W. but that he was not then at home. I kept the above note, and gave it to my cousin Dr. P. Hogan, V. G., of the diocess of Limerick, who I believe holds it still in possession. The Rev. P. Hogan, and another clergyman, kept a strict watch upon him for about three days, lest he might apostatize, until I went to Dr. Tuohy, upon his visitation, to have the suspension removed. In about six weeks after, the Rev. W. Hogan had some misunderstanding with the Rev. P. Hogan, with whom he lived as coadjutor; and in consequence of this difference, the Rev. W. Hogan mentioned to me, that he would again make application to Dr. Warburton for a living as Protestant minister: the result of this threat was, that Dr. Tuohy and Dr. P.

Hogan had to use extreme caution to prevent the Rev. William Hogan from apostatizing then.

"I am, &c. &c.
[*Signed.*] "G. D. HOGAN.
"One of the R. C. Clergymen at Conewago Church, Adams County, Pennsylvania."

"Lancaster City, *ss.*

"The Rev. G. D. Hogan being duly sworn according to law, deposeth and saith, that the foregoing as stated is correctly true, to the best of his knowledge and belief; and further saith not.

[*Signed.*] "G. D. HOGAN."
"Sworn and subscribed the 1st of March, 1821, before me.
[*Signed.*] "SAMUEL CARPENTER, *Alderman.*"

"P. S. In reading the third pamphlet of the Rev. William Hogan, I see a reiteration of his aspersions on the clergy of Philadelphia, maliciously derogating from their reputation as men of talents. It may not be amiss to apprise the public, that the learned gentleman's (William Hogan) almost '*miraculous*' course of theology did not exceed ten months; and that the sermon on the Festival of All Saints, which he obtruded on them as his own production, was given him by the Rev. Justin McNamara, of Cork, with many other sermons.

[*Signed.*] "G. D. H."

Among the fellow-passengers alluded to in one of the foregoing letters was Isaac Brown Parker, Esq., one of

Carlisle's most prominent and opulent citizens, who though a non-Catholic was always warmly identified with the interests of the Catholic Church. To strike up a casual acquaintance was unavoidable, if not a necessity, when we take the mode of travel customary in those days into consideration. Mr. Parker must have heard the heated discussion,—but since the confidential part of it was discussed in Gaelic (Irish) and not intended for the fellow-travelers, he may have been more charmed by the enphony of the language than interested in the burning questions discussed. William Hogan appealed to him for a sworn statement to rebut the evidence of his adversary and elicited the following reply.

"Cumberland County, } *
Pennsylvania.

"Before the subscriber, one of the Judges of the court of Common Pleas, in and for the county of Cumberland, in the Commonwealth of Pennsylvania, personally came Isaac Brown Parker of the borough of Carlisle, Esq. who being duly sworn, doth depose and say as follows to wit: That on or about the 10th day of January last past, this deponent travelled in the public stage, from the city of Lancaster to the city of Philadelphia, in company among other passengers, with two gentlemen, whom this deponent subsequently learned, were the Reverend Messrs.

---

* *Brief Reply &c.* in the possession of the *Amer. Cath. Historical Society.*

William and George Hogan. That to him both gentlemen were and still are strangers ; but had in the course of the last summer or fall, seen or heard the latter person preach in the Roman Catholic chapel in the borough of Carlisle, and from that circumstance recollected his features. That the said two Reverend gentlemen on the way from Lancaster to Downington, occupied the front seat of the carriage, and this deponent sat upon the next adjoining seat, fronting them. That during the morning's ride in the dark, the conversation of those gentlemen was entirely confined to themselves, and was, as this deponent is impressed with belief, carried on in the Irish language,

"This deponent is unable to state what the particular subject or topick of their conversation was ; but after daylight and breakfast, the intercourse and conversation with the other passengers on the part of the Reverend William Hogan, became more general and social, and this deponent, from attending to his observations, and deportment, formed an impression favourable to him as a gentleman and a scholar of sound erudition ; and frequently took the liberty of replying to his remarks, and extending the conversation. That in no part of the journey, within the knowledge and observation of this deponent, was the conduct, or conversation of the Reverend William Hogan in any manner unbecoming the character of a gentleman, a Christian, or a teacher of the Catholic faith ; but on the contrary was polite, courteous, edifying and agreeable to his fellow-passengers—and certainly at no time during the journey did it occur to this deponent, that any displeasure was evinced, or any remonstrance, by any of the passengers, against the deportment or conversation of the said Reverend gentleman. This deponent further states, in justice to both gentlemen,* that their deportment and conversation was such as highly became their sacred stations, and their bearings to each other, marked with friendly attentions and mutual cordiality.

[*Signed.*] "I. B. PARKER."

"*Sworn and subscribed the 17th day of March, A. D. 1821, before me,*

[*Signed.*] "JAMES ARMSTRONG."

---

* One of Hogan's abettors, and one who championed his erratic conduct with considerable skill and effectiveness, was Rev. Thaddeus J. O'Meally. His pamphlet entitled "An Address Explanatory and Vindicatory," (Phila., 1824,) covering 81 closely, printed pages, only widened the breach already existing between the Bishop and his flock. Of course he was suspended, and persisting to officiate at St. Mary's after his inhibition was excommunicated. He went to Rome to plead his cause in person. Rome pointed out the error of his scandalous conduct, and insisted upon a public recantation to be signed by him and published in this country. He made his submission, and did all he could to make amends and atone for his disobedience and rebellion—and sent on the following recantation which reached Bishop Conwell at Carlisle † on one of his episcopal visitations, where he had it published. We reprint it; it runs as follows:—

"DECLARATION."

"I the undersigned, Thaddeus Joseph O'Meally, priest of the diocess of Limerick, in Ireland, residing for some time past in Philadelphia, North America, understanding the perversity of my conduct, by joining to support the schismatical faction of certain trustees of St. Mary's Church, the cathedral of that city, in usurping the prerogatives of a pastor of said church, in defiance of the bishop's mandate to the contrary, to the great scandal of the surrounding nations, especially to that of America, and sincerely

† Dr. England's *Work*, Section 28, p. 201,

This, as far as Carlisle is concerned, ends the career of Father George Hogan. His last entry in the Church Records is dated July 7th, 1822. According to the personal memorandum kept by Bishop Neumann, he secured his *exeat*, left for France, and died in Paris the same year.

As for William Hogan and the schism he inaugurated, we shall encounter its malign and deadly work in the next chapter.

AN EPISODE.

FATHER HOGAN AND CHIEF JUSTICE GIBSON.

It was during the pastorate of Father Hogan, that an episode occurred treasured up by tradition with mingled feelings of indignation and admiration,—an instance of

---

lamenting my misconduct on that occasion; and, truly penitent for the scandal originating from that source, I am now anxious to repair the evils I have committed, as much as lies in my power; for which purpose I now publicly profess and proclaim to the world, that I have renounced forever the said faction, and their schismatical proceedings, and that I have abdicated accordingly the usurped right of pastorship in St. Mary's, conformably to the apostolical instructions contained in the *brief* of His Holiness, Pope Pius the Seventh, of sanctified memory, dated the 24th of August, 1822, and imploring pardon and forgiveness from the Most Reverened Father in God, Henry Conwell, Bishop of Philadelphia, for all the transgressions which I have committed against his authority, begging at the same time from him, or from the Holy See, to be absolved from the major excommunication which the bishop had inflicted on me with every degree of justice on his part. And I hereby solemnly swear to abide forever by the profession which I now make; and that I shall never, upon any account whatsoever, return again into the diocess of Philadelphia, and that a perpetual monument of this, my steadfast resolution and purpose may forever exist and be recorded, I have subscribed my name to this declaration, anxious that it be printed, in order that the knowledge of it may be diffused and universally published to the world.

[*Signed*.] "THADDEUS JOSEPH O'MEALLY.
"Rome, 25 July, 1825."

heartless brutality, on the one hand, and the most humane benevolence, on the other. The sequel is almost as strange as the occurrence itself.

It appears that Father Hogan, with the scant pecuniary assistance derived from his church revenue, was in such financial straits as to be unable to defray the expenses of his boarding house account. The two weeks he usually spent in Carlisle, found him lodged with a Mr. M. The hospitality which every Catholic would consider the highest honor to exercise, it seems was the occasion of a most dastardly insult on the part of M.,—who, by the way, was a man of some consequential importance in his own little world—being a constable. His action gives the keynote to the sincerity and stability of his faith.

It was a time when the "debtor's act" was in full force—a relic of savage barbarism, which was enforced with a pitiless inhumanity, the recollections of which should make us hang our heads in shame and confusion. "No crime known to the law brought so many to jails and prisons as the crime of debt, and the class most likely to get into debt was the most defenceless and dependent." * * * * Father Hogan was not in a position to pay his account. Mr. M. had recourse to the law,—and, serving the writ himself, was taking the poor priest to a debtor's cell

---

* *McMaster, Hist. of the People of the United States. Vol. I.*, p. 98. For a full description of this law in force, see the same work. Pp. 99-100.

to join the vagabonds, thieves and criminals who had fallen into the clutches of the law.

The sight of a priest in the custody of the local Dogberry naturally aroused widespread attention. Street gamins, corner idlers (a genus still inextinct) followed in large and noisy crowds. Two gentlemen strolling leisurely along Hanover street, could not fail but be attracted by the large concourse of people, and upon making inquiry, were told half-gleefully, half-maliciously that " they were taking the Catholic priest to jail." One of them breaking through the mob, which made respectful way for him, his towering form receiving additional height by the passion of indignation which thrilled his very being,— he approached the redoubtable peacemaker, made a few inquiries, ascertained the amount of indebtedness, paid it then and there, and in scathing words and withering contempt personally conducted the mortified priest from the startled and disappointed mob, and sent the constable slinking home like a whipped cur. The man who did this, and the memory of whose deed is enshrined in the hearts of all Catholics in Carlisle, was the *Hon. John Bannister Gibson*, Chief Justice of Pennsylvania, one of the most erudite and profound jurists, one of the most accomplished and versatile scholars of his age. Of course, the relief of the priest and the gratitude of his flock was as pathetic as the discomfiture of M. was crushing.

To the Catholic mind, it was more than a mere fortuitous coincidence that subsequently two of Chief Justice Gibson's children—Mrs. Gen. R. H. Anderson and Col. George Gibson, U.S.A., became members of the Church. The present beautiful marble High Altar is a memorial to Col. Gibson, who, in addition to an honored and brilliant military career, led a most edifying life and died a most consoling death. A most tasteful tablet of brass, a tribute from the officers of his regiment, conspicuously placed in the church, attests the reverence and affection they bore him in life.

Perhaps it was more than a pure accident again—that when Mr. M. on his deathbed clamored for a priest—though the utmost expedition was exercised in despatching messengers to Chambersburg and York, duty had called them elsewhere, so that he died without the consolation of Holy Church.

CHAPTER X.

FATHER DWEN ASSUMES CHARGE OF THE CONGREGATION, AND CONTROLS ITS DESTINY FOR FIFTEEN YEARS. HE BECOMES VERY POPULAR AND INFUSES NEW LIFE INTO THE PARISH. TOUCHING OBITUARIES FROM THE YORK AND CARLISLE PAPERS.

Father Hogan's sojourn was too brief to leave more than a mere pleasant recollection on the part of the Carlisle

Catholics, of having had the consolation of a resident pastor with all the graces and blessings that are inseparably connected with his holy office, and on Father Hogan's part, perhaps, the not too agreeable impressions formed of a country that to him was undemonstrative, inhospitable, and ultra-democratic. He evidently never reconciled himself to the primitive mode of life, the chronic impecuniosity, the constrained intercourse, which only increased the unenviable lot of physical hardship and privation that was the heritage of every priest entering upon the American mission. His ministry, however, had the result of forming the scattered and disintegrating congregation into a more concrete and efficient body, and of reclaiming many who, strangers to sacramental grace for years, and living in an atmosphere impregnated with suspicion, if not hostility to the Church, had lapsed into a state of mere formal adherence,—the border land of apostasy. His successor, however, was a more plastic character, and adapted himself so readily and completely to the new life he was obliged to lead, that his career proved a most fruitful one, and even after the lapse of more than half a century, his memory is held in reverence and benediction.

Rev. Patrick Joseph Dwen was born at Shrowlon, Parish of Athy, County Kildare, Ireland, in 1795. He made his studies, both preparatory and theological, in Ireland, and like Father Hogan, came here fully prepared to enter the holy priesthood. He came to this country in 1821, and after a short probation, early in 1822, was ordained to the priesthood by Bishop Conwell, being one of the first aspirants that he raised to that dignity. Immediately after his ordination, the departure of Father Hogan causing a vacancy, he was appointed to succeed him as pastor of Carlisle and York. He came to Carlisle, July 20, 1822.

A better selection could hardly have been made. Physically a man of athletic build and vigorous constitution, full of youthful enthusiasm and unquenchable zeal, the arduous labors and wearisome journeyings of the mission were a mere bagatelle to him. Endowed with magnetic social qualities, always scrupulously exercised within the limits of gentlemanly propriety,—bubbling over with scintillating Hibernian wit, which never overstepped the borders of priestly decorum, he was readily admitted to Carlisle society, in which he was looked upon as both an acquisition and an ornament. Filled with a broad charity, which disarmed intolerance, silenced sectarian asperities, gained the hearts of all,—he became a potent factor in creating a more intelligent comprehension of the Church and broadening the lines of Christian fellowship. His social intercourse without obtruding the spirit of polemics or controversy,—softened the erroneous and unjust impressions harbored in the hearts of many, impressions which could not have been dislodged by any other medium. Without deviating one tittle from the allegiance he owed his Church, or sacrificing even a shadow of the dignity due his exalted calling, by his scholarly, at times half jocular badinage and his agreeable, but always circumspect deportment, he gained the goodwill and hearts of all who came in contact with him. It was by these suave and engaging methods more than theological wranglings or pulpit hot-shot, that he moulded public opinion with rare tact and diplomacy, so that a most liberal, humane, charitable feeling leavened the entire religious community. Carlisle's reputation at this time was not only that of the centre of social life, intellectual activity, broad culture,—but the most liberal and tolerant views on religion.

Father Dwen at once realized that to make his work effective and enduring, he would be obliged to be in close communication with his people. With this object in view, he had the congregations of York and Carlisle detached from Conewago, and apportioned as one parish. This without for a moment rupturing the pleasant intercourse with the mother house,—which continued to feel and show unabated interest in the welfare of its old affiliations, and gave every aid to the new pastor.

It was with this object in view Father Dwen effected a permanent settlement in Carlisle, and established his home about a block from the church, occupying the house now numbered 66 on East Pomfret St., the property then belonging to Barney Carney. Here he lived for many years.

His domestic arrangements at that time were presided over by his sister Anastasia, who marrying James Kiernan, (July 22, 1828,) was succeeded by a facetious character named Biddy Logue, who following the matrimonial precedent established in the modest ecclesiastical household—soon became the wife of a Mr. Sommerville.

Serving Carlisle and York conjointly, Father Dwen usually alternated between the two places, devoting two weeks to each. The presence of an active priest, with attractive social qualities and no little eloquence as a preacher, soon made itself felt,—and the little church was uncomfortably filled on the Sundays he spent in Carlisle, so that the necessity of enlarging soon became an imperative duty. In 1823, as will be seen later, the attempted enlargement began, only to end in discord, disruption and litigation. By the rights vested in Trustees, by the laws and customs of those days, Father Dwen was powerless to act,—though an inflexible determination and resolute purpose on his part to bring an end to the parochial broil,—of which more shall be heard,—would have been highly conducive to the peace of the congregation and the authority of the pastor. However, the annex to the Church was finally completed and dedicated in August, 1825, by Bishop Conwell, assisted by Rev. Bernard Keenan, Lancaster, Pa., Father Dwen, and presumably some of the Conewago fathers.

The social qualities of the new pastor, his intimate associations with the more intelligent portion of non-Catholics, had the result of forming a new clientage which was both a friend to the pastor and an aid to the Church. This was seen in 1828 when Father Dwen took an active and successful part in forming the "Catholic Association of America" in Carlisle, enlisting the lively sympathy and generous cooperation of its most prominent citizens, who being almost all of Irish extraction, though not Catholics, were equally impelled by motives of patriotism, to assist in wresting Catholic Emancipation from reluctant and tyrannous England. A separate chapter details this incident of local history.

After this no incident worthy of note occured in Carlisle during his pastorate. The congregation under his wise administration and prudent foresight, became unified and zealous. The rising generation for the first time received that methodic instruction in Catholic doctrine and practice, that could not fail to lay the foundation for its future permanency and stability and make it a worthy exponent of its higher life and more lofty spiritual aims. The absence of this proper initiation into Catholic teachings, while it seemed to affect the adult population to no appreciable extent,— for with them the foundation of faith was laid deep and strong,—had a most disastrous effect on the youthful portion of the small flock. Nor should we underestimate the potent influence exercised by Father Dwen on those at variance with Catholic faith. His intellectual endowments, his executive capacity, his force of character, his singleness of purpose, his unselfish devotion to his arduous work, left an impression that gained the admiration of all, and reflected a most flattering light on the priesthood. With such a leader Catholicity could not fail to gain the respect of even those whose church affiliation diverged most widely from it, and at the same time the heartiest recognition of its grateful children.

About the year 1830, Father Dwen changed his residence to York. This was no doubt rendered imperative by its increasing Catholic population and the more successful strides it had made in industrial prosperity. But his attachment for Carlisle was ever strong and sincere. With a regularity that knew no interruption, and a zeal that showed no moderation, he paid his fortnightly visit to Carlisle; the inclemency of the weather, the execrable condition of the roads, the premonitory symptoms of impaired health, could not check his ardor nor cool his sense of duty. Sick calls, especially, were responded to with a cheerful alacrity, though covering a territory of thirty or forty miles, and more than aught else pointed out the true shepherd of his flock. His management of the York parish proved him to have been a man of piety and tact. The congregation there had a strong contingent of Germans, and not being familiar with their language or customs, it is a matter of much surprise how he made the national foibles and jealousies obliterate themselves, when the practice of their faith was concerned. The harmony and good feeling that prevailed was as much the result of the holy example he gave as that of exercising a discretionary tact and conciliatory prudence that could not fail to arouse admiration and enkindle affection. With his mixed congregation united he had no difficulty in making church improvements. When he enlarged his church in 1832, by an addition of 15 feet, the work was not only speedily accomplished, but promptly paid for.

After his removal to York, he usually made his home while in Carlisle with Mrs. P. Gillen, where a most motherly hospitality awaited him, and where he always found that affectionate care and gentle ministration, when the ravages of sickness were undermining his rugged constitution, that gave it the warmth and comfort of a home.

Late in 1837 his health showed alarming indications of enfeeblement, which, while it caused anxiety to his friends, seemed to affect him very little. Unmindful of the injunctions of his physician, disregarding the stronger evidence of his malady's encroachment, he labored on with a courage that can only be called foolhardy. With prudence on his part, a cessation of his wearying journeys, and a careful compliance with the simplest hygienic laws, he might have been spared many years of usefulness and attained a ripe age. But with indomitable zeal there was found blended in his character a dogged obstinacy, which derided all fears and lent a deaf ear to all kind remonstrance. On February 3d, 1838, he officiated at Carlisle for the last time —and it was to be the last time that he would ever see it. His condition was such that he was obliged to be relieved of the work of attending Carlisle, in the hopes that by confining his labors to York alone, his recuperative powers, which had sustained him through a career of hardship, worry, and privation, would again assert themselves as they had done often before. His hopes were delusive and his illness was rapidly assuming a fatal termination, which finally came on February 7th, 1838.

The death was a sore blow to his people, whom he served with the most fatherly care and unswerving fidelity for more than fifteen years. His many virtues as a priest gained him the affectionate and enduring love of his flock: his manliness of character and rare social traits commanded the esteem of all whom he came in contact with. His early death was a heavy loss to the diocese, at a time when more than ever there was a crying demand for priestly ministration. To the present day, the name of Father Dwen is still a hallowed memory, one that invariably evokes with its recollection an affectionate eulogy on the part of non-Catholics, and a devout prayer on that of his old flock.

He was buried under St. Patrick's Church, York, Pa.,

where a neat, but modest tombstone perpetuates his memory in the following inscription:

> IN MEMORIAM
> REV. PATRICII J. DWEN
> PASTOR ISTIUS CONGREGATIONIS
> MIGRAVIT AD DOMINUM VII. FEB.
> ANNO SALUTIS MDCCCXXXVIII.
> ÆTATE SUA XLIII.
> ERECTED BY THE CONGREGATION.

(In Memory of Rev. Patrick J. Dwen, Pastor of this Congregation, Who went to his eternal reward Feb. 7, In the Year of Grace 1838, In the 43d year of his age. Erected by the Congregation.)

The following obituary notice appeared in the *York Gazette*:* "In being called on to record the death of Rev. Mr. Dwen, eulogy and panegyric seem superfluous, for, as the Pastor and Shepherd of his flock, his actions and deeds of charity are not written upon sand, but stand engraven upon the hearts of his parishioners. Fifteen years of his ecclesiastical life have been given to the people of his Church in the County of York, and whether among the rich or poor he was ever to be found ministering to the spiritual or temporal wants of his congregation. Amiability of deportment, polished manners, and perfect charity of feeling, have ever marked him out as the friend of man, as the companion of those who assented to his faith, or

---

* February 23d, 1838.

of those who may have differed from him in matters of religion.

"Beloved and regretted by *all*, he has passed from a world of care and temptation and trial, and gone to that haven of rest, prepared for the righteous 'who shall inherit the Kingdom of God.'"

A still more touching tribute, couched in terms both warm and eloquent, is the following, which appeared in the *Carlisle American Volunteer*, March 29, 1838, from a Protestant source, and which voiced the sentiments of non-Catholics about a man whom they all learned to revere and love.

"THE LATE REV. PATRICK J. DWEN.

"MESSRS. EDITORS: I observe by the late papers that this unobtrusive man, exemplary citizen and pious divine, has 'paid the debt of nature' and 'been gathered to his fathers,' while in the meridian of life and in the midst of his usefulness. For the past fifteen years he officiated as the Pastor of the Roman Catholic congregations of York and Carlisle, during which period he labored zealously and efficiently to promote both the spiritual and temporal welfare of the flocks committed to his charge. While he 'pursued the even tenor of his way' in inculcating and enforcing the doctrines of that church, in which he was educated and brought up, and impressing on his hearers the necessity of pursuing a strictly virtuous and religious life, he never gave offense to his dissenting brethren by assailing their different creeds or religious opinions. Unassuming in his manners, amiable in his disposition, courteous in his intercourse with his fellow-citizens, and his hand ever ready to extend relief to the suffering, he gained the esteem not only of his own flock, but of many *Protestants* with whom he had become acquainted, among whom was the humble writer of this brief obituary notice. He obeyed with alacrity the numerous calls of his congregation, at all hours, at all places, and under all circumstances, whether through tempests or calms, to administer the rites of his Church to the sick and dying. In thus obeying the calls of duty, which was in strict accordance with his own benevolent disposition, he but too frequently exposed himself to the 'pelting of the pitiless storm,' and thereby contracted a disease which gradually brought him from hence to another and better land. The deceased was a finished scholar, and well versed in the voluminous writings of the fathers and luminaries of the Church, but like too many other divines, he was no *pedant*, and it was therefore only those who were on terms of the strictest friendship and intimacy with him, that could properly appreciate his merits and talents. Being a native of the 'Emerald Isle,' and seeing and feeling the oppression of his country and countrymen, he became a naturalized citizen of his adopted country as soon as circumstances would permit, and upon all proper occasions exercised the inestimable right of suffrage, always supporting those whom he believed to be the most meritorious and competent candidates for public favor. It will no doubt be gratifying to his numerous friends here, as it certainly was to me, to know that his remains were attended to the silent tomb in the following order, as given in the *York Gazette*:

The Clergy.
Body—Borne by Eight Carriers.
Mourners and Pall-Bearers.
Officers of the Borough and Strangers.
Females.
The Congregation and Citizens.

"The body arriving at the church was placed upon a form covered over with white linen and having on it twelve tapers. During the celebration of the Mass the coffin remained open—the body was clothed with the dress of the priesthood, with white vestments. Mass was celebrated by the Rev. Mr. Maher, of Harrisburg, and the sermon and panegyric were delivered by the Rev. Mr. Dougherty, of Conewago. The discourse of Rev. Mr. Dougherty drew forth tears from every eye and sighs from every bosom. The panegyric was short, but it told all that could be told of the virtues and merits of the deceased. He spoke eloquently of the charities and kindness of Mr. Dwen, and of his humble and Christian deportment throughout life. After the Mass and Gospel had been read the priests went to the sacristy and laid aside their vestments and returned to perform the last offices for the dead. The obsequies being over the body was deposited in a vault prepared for it at the entrance into the sanctuary. The ceremonies throughout were impressive and solemn. The number of persons present could not have been less than two thousand in and around the church.

[SIGNED.] "FIAT JUSTITIA."

The words of the Apostle—"*Mihi mori lucrum,*"—"for me to die is gain," would have made a most fitting epitaph for Rev. P. J. Dwen.

CHAPTER XI.

THE HOGAN SCHISM—ITS DISASTROUS EFFECT ON THE CHURCH—THE HOGANITES HAVE THEIR BILL PASSED BY THE STATE LEGISLATURE—GOV. HIESTER VETOES IT—THE CARLISLE CONGREGATION TAKES AN ACTIVE PART IN UPHOLDING LEGITIMATE AUTHORITY—THE "RELIGIOUS QUESTION" IN POLITICS.

In a cursory way we touched upon the disorder and scandal caused by the usurpation of ecclesiastical authority on the part of the Trustees of Trinity Church, Philadelphia, in arbitrarily ousting Father Helbron and violating all canonical laws by installing Goetz in his place. The temporary success, then still a sad recollection in the memory of living man, and the aftermath of the soul-blighting conflict—for the scandal struck hard and deep—was apparently dying out, but there remained the smouldering embers of the old-timed disaffection, which only needed a crafty leader to make him a veritable firebrand in stirring the old rancor and animosity into a state of frenzied fierceness. It was the old story of lay pretension, bolstered by recalcitrant priests, autocratically dictatorial and blindly obstinate, arrayed against lawful ecclesiastical authority, tenacious of its prerogatives, unyielding in its maintenance of them, guarding its ancient immunities as a sacred trust that could not be tampered with. The brooding spirit of contumacy, openly and publicly renouncing allegiance to the Church, and antagonizing her authority in the spiritual domain, was not the new product of a new country. The battle had been waged and fought in every country where Christianity sought an asylum. She never issued from the conflict with trailing colors, nor would she do so in this instance. Only blind fanaticism and overweening vanity thought otherwise. To the Catholic they were trying and disheartening moments, but he knew the Church would issue from the conflict unscathed, purified, and her prestige more assured than before.

It was at the instance of Rev. George D. Hogan, whose career we have just touched upon, that his cousin, Rev. William Hogan, came to this country from Limerick, Ireland. After settling in New York (Albany) for a short time, upon the urgent representations of this relative, he was provisionally admitted to the Philadelphia Diocese.

Hogan was a man of conspicuously handsome person, of most suave and engaging manners, with rare and charming conversational gifts, a ready and eloquent preacher, a man who, could he have curbed a most inordinate vanity and passionate ambition, would have been on the highway to ecclesiastical preferment. His egotism and pride were unduly encouraged and pampered by an adulatory host of laymen who, whilst they admired his brilliant intellectual attainments, were blind to the absence of those virtues that more than aught else constitute the ideal priest. His conduct towards his Bishop, who lived in the same house with him—St. Mary's being the Cathedral church—was overbearing and disrespectful, though he was a mere object of sufferance in the diocese. When pride and vanity gave way to taunts and insults, of which his superior was the object and victim, the result looked ominous. But when finally he lent himself, the willing tool of the Trustees, to inveigle the faithful from their allegiance and make them hostile to their Bishop, and even alienate the church property to hold it themselves, then the outcome could readily be anticipated. The Bishop's course was prudent, tempered with mildness and forbearance—the battle waged against him, fierce, brutal, relentless. The story is too lengthy and too irrelevant for the scope of this work—further than showing the prompt and decisive action taken by the Carlisle congregation in upholding legitimate authority and vindicating the imperilled rights of the Church. Suffice it to state, however, that the Hoganites were daily drifting further and further from their Catholic moorings, until the line of demarcation between rampant heresy and loyal faith could no longer be distinguished. The attitude of these men against lawful authority was so stubbornly belligerent, so relentlessly acrimonious and so ruinously disastrous to faith and morals, that Bishop Conwell was at last compelled, by sheer stress of circumstances, to formally and publicly excommunicate Hogan and his abettors. Undeterred, the Trustees took possession of the church, drove away the Bishop, installed Hogan as pastor, and by this formal secession established an independent Catholic Church. New York, Norfolk, and Charleston, had in the meantime become tainted with these schismatical tendencies, always zealously propagated by the redoubtable Trustee, until it seemed the contagion would permeate the greater part of the ecclesiastical body. Not satisfied with this internecine strife, the courts were invoked and the legislature appealed to, to sustain the schismatics in their war of disruption. On March 20, 1823, a bill was introduced, passing both houses with mysterious celerity, giving a legal status to the Hoganites. Rabid fanaticism and frenetic bigotry could hardly wish for more.

The bill was entitled " A Supplement to an act entitled, An act to incorporate the members of the religious society of Roman Catholics belonging to the congregation of St. Mary's Church, in the city of Philadelphia, passed the thirteenth day of September, one thousand seven hundred and eighty-eight."

The bill was more insidious in its construction than sweeping in its enactments. As we saw, the church was incorporated in 1788 by the legislature, and the charter of incorporation provides that the officiating pastor should be "*duly appointed.*" This was the source of contention. Those who petitioned for an alteration in the charter, alleged that its proper construction if it did not assert the right of the pew-holders of the congregation to elect their pastor, as is done in other churches, was at least extremely doubtful, and therefore called for the interposition of the legislature to clear away the doubt, and make that certain by legislative enactment which was obscure.

The church authorities, on the other hand, maintained that the meaning of the words "*duly appointed*" was too obvious to admit of even a shadow of doubt; that it had reference to the immemorial custom in the Church, undeniable and incontrovertible, which invests the appointing power in the Bishop, and the obedience of the priests was a matter of Church discipline which the Church never deviated from.

The petitioners then took the characteristically Protestant view, and here the animus of their action became apparent, that it was contrary to the genius of our institutions and diametrically opposed to our laws to admit foreign jurisdiction over the property and conduct of American citizens,—that the refusal would be an implied recognition of papal authority in the State of Pennsylvania, inasmuch as in that event the Pope would continue to appoint the Bishop, and the Bishop the priest, and that both would thunder their fulminations and excommunications against every dissenting Catholic. On the other hand it was urged, that the alteration would be impolitic in the extreme,—that the States of the Union were emphatically the protectors of religion, and that its constitution recognized the rights of conscience and universal toleration ;—that by holding out this inducement with others, her shores had become the refuge of the oppressed and the asylum of the persecuted ; and that it would be more than deliberate cruelty to allure and seduce from foreign countries and then abandon to religious persecution the victims enticed.

Most cunningly framed, this bill would have made the clergy the tools of the Trustees,—altered the charter without the full consent of the congregation, disturbed and subverted fundamental articles of faith in contravention of Catholic practices. In short, it invested the Trustees with plenipotentiary powers as far as the goverument of the temporalities, appointment of pastors was concerned, —and delivered the Church, a fettered and manacled victim, into their hands. At this date it is a matter of surprise how perversity and obtuseness could go to such direful extremes, and were it not that it is a matter of historical record would stagger belief. Fortunately, Governor Joseph Hiester gave the agitation a momentary quietus by his strong and timely veto of March 27, 1823.

The Catholics in the State could not remain apathetic with such a calamity facing the Church. Before the passage of the bill, petitions rained in upon the legislature, and every means adopted to have it suppressed. Now that the Governor of the State came to their aid and championed the cause of justice and religious liberty, their hearts naturally went out to him in expressions of gratitude that would seem extravagant to those unaware of the consequences involved and the calamities averted. Carlisle and Lancaster were the first to grasp the situation, and would not allow the occasion to pass without voicing their sentiments, recording their protest, and giving utterance to their sense of gratitude. The promptness and thoroughness with which the Carlisle congregation did this, gives evidence not only of an unswerving faith and trusting loyalty, but at the same time of a most commendable zeal and high order of intelligence.*

---

* There is a lurking suspicion in the mind of the writer that the following letter was drafted by Richard Dougherty, a typical Irish schoolmaster of the old school, who was famous in his day as a classical scholar of a high order, a brilliant raconteur, and an ambulating encyclopædia of quaint and archaic lore. His limping walk and deftness in handling the birch are still vividly remembered by his old pupils—especially the latter.

In the Carlisle *American Volunteer* * this card appeared:

"CATHOLIC QUESTION."

"The members composing the Catholic Congregation of the borough of Carlisle are earnestly requested to meet at their place of worship, at two o'clock P. M., on Saturday, the 12th instant, for the purpose of expressing their *public thanks* to the Governor of the State, and the Representatives of the people *who* had *the official* and constitutional fidelity and justice to protect the *Rights of Conscience and Chartered Immunities*, against the contemplated violation of *religion, law*, and the constitution of the land.

      [*Signed*] CORMICK MCMANUS, ⎫
                BERNARD CARNEY, ⎬ Trustees.
                WALTER E. ERWIN, ⎭

"Carlisle, April 2."

The result of the meeting is given in the *Volunteer* of April 17th, and we will let the paper tell the rest:

"THE MEETING

"Of the *Catholic congregation* of the borough of *Carlisle*, after having been organized by appointing *Cormick*

---

* April 3, 1823.

McManus as chairman, and *Richard Dougherty* and *John Faust* as secretaries, *unanimously* adopted the following proceedings:

"PREAMBLE.

"Cited by the above call, and in cheerful obedience to it, the *Catholic congregation* of this church have met, at the *time* and *place* assigned, for the grateful and meritorious purposes therein specified, and after a deliberate interchange of opinions upon this serious and interesting subject, it was *unanimously* recommended and acquiesced in, that a respectful *letter of thanks* be addressed to Joseph Hiester, Esq., Governor of Pennsylvania, for the firm, dignified, and liberal protection with which he shielded *The Great Constitutional Question of Religious and Chartered Rights*, by his correct and comprehensive *veto*, upon the innovating, improvident, and *unconstitutional bill*, passed by both branches of the legislature of this State, to alter the charter of St. Mary's church of the city of Philadelphia—a bill sweeping into destruction at one and the same time, *defined and specific contracts of laws and imprescriptible rights of conscience;* nor ought our gratitude and religious feelings ever cease to embalm the memory of those enlightened and faithful Representatives of both Houses, who virtuously combatted this *monstrous bill* in every step of its iniquitous march."

"LETTER OF THANKS."

To His Excellency, Joseph Hiester, Governor of Pennsylvania:

SIR,—We all, thank God, live in a country and under laws which have put the mark of *Cain* upon two of the fell and impious instruments of the *prince of darkness—Bigotry and Religious Intolerance.* The *furious fanatic* may foam, and the *fiery zealot* rave, but their inability to injure has given to *Persecution* its *death stab*, and suspends it before the enlightened eye of mankind, as a hideous object of indignation, derision and scorn. Eternal thanks to the *immortal revolutionary founders* of this *great Republic*, for such celestial and transcendant blessings! Here too, in this glorious land of *religious toleration*, the profligate *libertine* and the impious latitudinarian are chained down by the sublime and awful edicts of both National and State constitutions, from perpetrating an indiscriminate *vandalism* upon *religious worship*, and prostrating at their unholy feet, that filial and affectionate *duty* which *piety* owes to its canonical enactments. The principles, and professions, and practice of the *Roman Catholic Faith*, are immutable—universal—eternal—uniform all over the world, in every practice, of both its *creed* and *discipline*, never veering to the seductions or delusions of either fancy, infidelity, or caprice; it is founded even in its most minute decrees and observances upon the acquiescence and allegiance, in every age, of its holy, revered and illustrious professors, from the *saint* to the *pilgrim*, from the *mitred head* to the most humble, illiterate secular—from the *prince* to the *beggar*. A faith thus piously obedient and nobly consistent; thus fixed and exact; thus sublimely peculiar and singular in all its relations; thus based upon Christian foundation, of nearly two thousand years' standing, and *constitutionally protected* in this Republic, to the very extent and plenitude of its *exercise*, should not be mocked or insulted, by *any enactment of Legislative caprice*, or *infidel ribaldry;* should not be imposed upon the reckless and heartless innovation, of an *unconstitutional* and *spoliating law*, altering the *religious rights* and *charter* of St. Mary's Church. Let it not be said we are strangers, and no party to this unfortunately agitated question. It is a *Catholic* question, it is *universal* in its nature and an infringement and usurpation upon the *canonical* institutions and ordinances of *that faith*, in whatever region from pole to pole, that this faith is professed. Accept, then, sir, we respectfully pray you, the sincere and grateful thanks of this meeting, for that magnanimity and firmness, with which you extinguished, by an honest and virtuous *veto*, the *unconstitutional* and *violent* bill passed to alter the charter of St. Mary's Church. And however honorably the constitution may have borne you out, in the judicious exercise of that high and wholesome power, with which it has wisely invested you, it would be an ungenerous and illiberal apathy on our part, and a frozen evidence of utter insensibility, to view in silence, the bright and saving banner which you have displayed over the *Security of Religious Exercise And The Inviolability Of Its Chartered Rights.* And it only adds to the reputation of your firmness and official vigilance, that you have destroyed *this licentious and demoralizing* bill, at that important and responsible post, assigned to your care, ere it reached the formidable barriers of the *judiciary*, where it would finally and inevitably perish beneath the austere and portentous frowns of that *August Tribunal.*

"Signed in behalf of the meeting.

CORMICK MCMANUS,
BERNARD CARNEY,   } *Trustees.*
WALTER R. ERWIN,

"*Resolved*, That the virtuous and enlightened Representatives of the Houses of the Legislature who opposed the bill, altering the charter of St. Mary's Church, receive the cordial thanks of this meeting for the zeal, fidelity and talents with which they defended *religious rights* and *chartered compacts.*

"*Resolved*, That the meeting disclaim all intention of creating any political ferment, for party purposes, out of this subject, and earnestly recommend their Catholic brethren throughout the State to confer their votes, upon all occasions, upon merit, morals and qualifications only, and to be guided solely in the exercise of their suffrages by patriotic views and virtuous predilections.

"*Resolved*, That these proceedings be published throughout the State by such editors of newspapers as are friendly to the cause of truth and justice.

"*Resolved*, That the Trustees of this congregation forward these proceedings to the Governor and retain a copy of them in the archives of the church.

CORMICK MCMANUS, *Chairman.*

[*Signed*] RICHARD DOUGHERTY, } *Secretaries.*
JOHN FAUST,

The open letter of the Carlisle and Lancaster congregations, in giving expression to that feeling which every Catholic would have considered his bounden duty to express as a just appreciation of conduct on the part of Governor Hiester—a conduct that was more than diplomatic in being simply heroic, was wantonly misconstrued, ruthlessly dragged into the political arena, and made the campaign of 1823, for Governor, more than customarily bitter and fierce. The contending parties were the Federalists and Democratic-Republicans. Hiester was a candidate for re-election, and aside of the dignified and brave standpoint he took in vetoing the bill above alluded to, was a man of brilliant attainments and unswerving honesty. His opponent, Schulze, though his character could not be impugned—was the son of a Lutheran minister, and himself for six years followed the same avocation until physical disability made him exchange the clerical for a mercantile career. But what aroused the antagonism and indignation of Catholics, was his advocacy of the bill which the foregoing letter so scathingly denounces.

The papers which at that time devoted nearly all their available space to politics, which was discussed with a vehemence and acerbity highly amusing to us of the present day, took up the matter, and for several weeks the "Catholic Question" was thoroughly ventilated. F. P. Schwarz, who was the editor of the *Sunbury Enquirer*, and a Catholic of very liberal tendencies, judging from his editorial utterances, precipitated matters by keeping alive this religio-political campaign.

As usual in such cases where the Church is dragged into the heat of political discussion,—it was productive of heaping contumely on her, and subjecting its members to an incessant fusilade of invective,—whilst the political demagogues carried their ends. The Hiester-Schulze campaign however had aroused the Catholic mind to the iniquitous proceedings of the Philadelphia Trustees, to the inadequacy and danger of the entire Trustee system, and the disastrous results of antagonizing the centre of Catholic unity—authority. In bringing about this consummation the loyal faith, alert watchfulness and timely intervention of the congregations outside of Philadelphia, had not a little to do, and the fact that Carlisle was one of the first if not the first to take the initiative, redounds not a little to its credit.

At this date we cannot fail to take a pardonable pride in having an ancestry of such sterling faith, which had the grasp of mind to gauge the menacing features of the question, and had the intellectual qualifications to formulate a protest, the diction of which though it may appear somewhat stilted,—conceals a clinching logic all the same, both comprehensive and irrefragable.

The Hoganite Schism in due time came to an end. After eking out an adventurous and precarious existence for seven years, its impotent fight ceased, not, however, before Rome had on three several times condemned it, and many souls had been lost. Hogan left the church,—and was visited by summary punishment, swift and relentless,—he married two widows,—was lost from public notice,—and died in poverty and obscurity.

The unfortunate struggle is to be deplored,—but it gave the deathblow to a most pernicious system.

CHAPTER XII.

BUILDING OF THE CHURCH.—THE TRUSTEES COME TO COLLISION.—THE CARNEY IMBROGLIO.—NEWSPAPER CONTROVERSY.—CARNEY COLLECTS SUBSCRIPTIONS AND PEW RENTS BY LAW.—HE DIES OUT OF THE CHURCH.

Since the erection of the old church in 1806, Catholicity had made considerable strides in ways and importance that augured most auspiciously for the future. The gain was not only in numerical strength, but also in social recognition and solid prosperity. The members were daily becoming more imbued not only with the privileges of their citizenship, but also with that impulsive American progressiveness—which already was a marvel to Europe. Endowed by nature with a robust constitution, inured to hardship from infancy, gifted with keen and sturdy honesty, the emigrant of years ago was gradually becoming no inconsequential factor in public life. This marked advance was felt and noticed in Carlisle. Already some of our prominent tradesmen and contractors were found among the Catholics,—and even the poor laboring men though still in a majority, in spite of the beggarly pittance they earned—three to four dollars a week,—were men who enjoyed the confidence and esteem of their employers.

In 1822 we find *thirty-nine* pew holders crowded in the little church without adverting to the women, adults and children of the congregation. How they ever gained even the merest admission, not to speak of accommodation is a problem, the solution of which taxed the minds of the Trustees as much then, as its contemplation puzzles us now. No doubt the renting of the pews was a mere formal proceeding to insure a suitable revenue, whilst the most liberal, communistic ideas prevailed as to their occupancy. The visits of the attending priest and his semi-monthly sojourn in their midst helped not only to increase the number of attendants at service,—but more than ever urged the necessity of enlarged accommodation.

The first step in this direction, taken with evident hesitancy was voiced in the following memorandum in the "Church Records:"

"SUNDAY, July the 21st, 1822."

"At a meeting of the members of the Roman Catholic Church of Carlisle, held on this day in said church, to take into consideration and adopt regulations for the Provision of a Clergyman, and also to elect four Trustees for the ensuing year.—After the election of the Trustees, the following resolution was adopted as follows:

"That two additional pews be erected in front of the existing ones at the expense of the congregation, and that the whole should be rented by the Trustees to the members, and the proceeds, with the rent of the house belonging to the Church to be given to the Revd. Mr. Dwen as his yearly salary, for his services as clergyman of said church.

"The Pews to consist of Twenty in number, the front Pews to rent for $13. a pair, the succeeding ones to fall 1 dollar each, which will amount to $170., with the rent of the dwelling house in addition, which will be $26., making in all the sum of $196. yearly.

  Trustees for the year,   CORMICK MCMANUS
             BERNARD CARNEY,
 [*Signed.*]   WM. CRAMOR,
             WALTER R. ERWIN."

The pew holders in 1822 who were to pay their rent quarterly to the Trustees, who in turn handed it over to Father Dwen, were the following:

Right Aisle	Left Aisle
Walter R. Erwin	Bernard Carney
John Gillen	Francis McManus
Patrick Philips	Edward Higgins
Patrick McGuire	Patrick Derson (Dawson)
Cormick McManus	Mr. Waters
John Faust	Hugh McCormick
N. Gingly	James McIntire
Peter Black	Mr. Sigler
Miss Inders	Mr. Cramor
John Monks	Patrick Boyle
Michael Dawson	Michael Boyle
Peter Gilmore	Edward Friel
Lewis Rancilear	Ch. Callaughan
Thompson Brown	John Carney
Patrick Smith	Ed. McLeary
Patrick McManus	Edward White
Charles McManus	
Patrick McAuly	
Richard Dougherty	
Dominick Corny	
Joseph Smith	
John Higgins	

The additional two pews were totally inadequate to supply the demand for seats,—a cry that became more clamorous—the longer Father Dwen exercised his ministry in the parish. No doubt what seemed to the Trustees a most formidable undertaking, was to him a crying necessity, when he saw the crowded condition of the church and had to officiate in a suffocatingly contracted little room. The venture to enlarge the church was fully discussed during the following winter and only one of two remedies seemed adequate to a proper solution, and that was either a new or an enlarged Church. The latter was decided upon, as the following advertising card in the Carlisle paper* bears witness :—

"NOTICE"

"TO CARPENTERS, BRICKLAYERS AND PLASTERERS.

" Sealed proposals will be received by the Trustees of the Roman Catholic Church, Carlisle, for the erecting of an additional building to the present church, of 58 ft. by 30, and 21 ft. high to the square. Those wishing to take on the work, can see the plan of said building by calling on

[Signed.]   BARNEY CARNEY,
               CORMICK MCMANUS, } *Trustees.*
               WALTER R. ERWIN,

---

* *American Volunteer*, March 16, 1823.

"Those intending to contract for said work will send in their Proposals on the 17th of March at the hour of 10 o'clock in the forenoon, at the Union Hotel, where the Trustees will attend for that purpose."

The work begun under such favorable circumstances was not only doomed to more than a year's delay,—but was the origin of what, for want of a better name, we may call the Carney imbroglio. Trustees, with the onerous responsibilities of governing the Church, like the redoubtable specimens above alluded to, were no doubt duly impressed with the importance of their office—but when it came to internal friction and strife, one would think that policy would prompt them, from personal if not religious motives, to maintain harmony by amicably adjusting their difficulties and burying their resentments, and above all to avoid the scandal of making public exhibitions of their grievances and misunderstandings. Unfortunately our Trustees rushed into print, made their quarrels common property, and most effectually, for the time being at least, put a summary stop to the work on the incomplete church. It took nearly three years to accomplish what, with unity of action under skillful guidance, could have been done in six months. Not to allude to the scandal and disaster this difficulty caused in the congregation, it shook the confidence of non-Catholic benefactors. The only feature worthy of some consideration in this quarrel was that its ventilation in the public prints enables the narrative of the annex building to be accurately given,—for the Church Records give us not a scintilla of information about the affair.

The story runs that Barney Carney, one of the supplanted Trustees, for at the annual election new ones had been elected, was either improvident or dishonest in handling the church funds. It is not our province to sift the conflicting and meagre evidence. The newly elected Trustees, upon their accession, discovered the supposed discrepancy, and demanded books, receipts, bills, etc., from Carney. His refusal, and the fact that he was no longer a member of the Board of Trustees, prompted them to issue the following advertisement :*

" TAKE NOTICE.

" All persons who have subscribed money to the Trustees of the Roman Catholic Church of the borough of Carlisle, either here or elsewhere, are requested *not to pay it to Bernard Carney*, or any person else without the authority of the undersigned Trustees of said church. In testimony whereof we hereunto subscribe our names, this 16th day of February, 1824.

[*Signed.*]   JOHN GILLEN,   }
         EDWARD HAGAN, } *Trustees.*
         PETER GILMORE, }

---

*American Volunteer, February 19, 1824.

Thus challenged, Carney had but two alternatives to protect his impugned honesty,—either by seeking redress at law, or availing himself of a public vindication in the newspaper. He did the latter—and for more than six consecutive issues (weekly) of the *Volunteer*, immediately below the above notice, stands Carney's counterblast :

"*To all that subscribed towards the erection of an additional building to the Roman Catholic Church of Carlisle:*

"The present Trustees of said church, having thought proper, in an advertisement, to request said subscribers not to pay me their subscriptions ; I therefore inform said subscribers, and *particularly request*, that they pay no money or moneys to the present Trustees, as the subscription book has been transferred to me for collection. I have contracted for the building for the sum of $1,450, and the only security I have for said sum is the subscription book, the money subscribed in which I must collect myself. I have expended on said building $115.75½ more than I have collected, which appeared on settlement, and was acknowledged by said Trustees. I therefore protest against the publication made by them. I submit the statement made, acknowledged and attested by Isaac Todd, Esq., and John Higgins.

"Amount of expenditure in favor of the Catholic Church in Carlisle by Barney Carney:

"Amount expended . . .	$765.38
" Do. received by collection .	652.70
"Balance due Carney . . .	112.63
"Necessary expenses on settlement	3.12½
	$115.75½

[Signed.]   "EDWARD HAGAN,
                  "JOHN GILLEN.

"Attest, JOHN HIGGINS,
        ISAAC TODD.

"In addition to the above sum, I am responsible for the payment of several hundred dollars.
   [Signed.]   "BARNEY CARNEY.
"February 19, 1824."

The struggle waxed warm,—but the congregation inclined more to sustain the Trustees than to vindicate Carney. The Trustees made an effort to collect some of the outstanding subscriptions, but as soon as Carney had an intimation of it, he had the following notice inserted in the *Volunteer*.*

---

* April 15, 1824.

"NOTICE.

"All persons who have subscribed towards the erection of the additional building of the *Roman Catholic Church of Carlisle*, are requested to pay me the amount of their subscriptions on Friday the 30th of April. I will attend at the house of John Stockdale in the borough of Carlisle, said day, from ten till twelve o'clock in the forenoon, and from two till four five o'clock in the afternoon, to receive payment. Those who do not comply with this request, will *without respect of persons*, be dealt with as the law directs, as I am the only person authorized to receive the same."

 [*Signed.*]   "BARNEY CARNEY.
"April 14, 1824."

This was no idle threat—for Carney was both impulsive and obstinate, and two days later promptly instituted suit against James Boyle and Michael Dawson, in the former case for a $5.00 subscription and a $3.00 order, in the latter case for $1.12½ pew rent and an $8.00 subscription. He entered judgment, which they waived, on the plea of insolvency—and he actually had *them put to jail under the debtors' act.*

The case appealed, the Court sustained Carney, and again* affairs assumed a most alarming attitude.

---

* See nos. 284, 285 286, April Term, 1824, C. P. Cumberland Co.

The pacific overtures of Father Dwen, and the conciliatory action of the old Trustees, headed by the prudent Cormick McManus, averted a calamity which might have resulted in irreparable spiritual harm. As it was, it retarded the work on the Church, closed the channels of charity, fomented discord, and was unquestionably the source of grave scandal.

As a final means of adjusting the difficulties it was concluded to submit them to the arbitration of some disinterested persons,—and consider the adjudication final. This was done by mutual consent, and an opinion unfavorable to Carney handed in. Exasperated beyond endurance Carney came out with the following manifesto:*

"TO THE PUBLICK.

"It is with regret, I feel bound in vindication of myself, to publish my protest against the decision or the arbitrators in the case of myself against Cormick McManus and Walter R. Erwin, former trustees of the Roman Catholic Church in Carlisle, published in the Carlisle *Herald* and *Gazette*. All I will say for the present is, I consider myself ungenerously and dishonorably dealt with, which I will make appear to the satisfaction of the public very shortly. It is true I signed an article to abide by the decision of the

---

* *American Volunteer*, June 20, 1824.

arbitrators appointed to settle the amount of moneys received and paid by me, on account of the Roman Catholic Church, but, there was not a word in said article nor did it come before the arbitrators, that I was to give up the building and receive nothing for a whole summer's attendance and lost time. It is therefore my intention to have justice done me fairly ; in doing so, the public will be the better acquainted with the treatment I have received from a set of *fellows*, who are well known for their deficiency and want of common sense and decency."

[*Signed.*] "BARNEY CARNEY"
" Carlisle. June 22, 1824."

Carney may have found some justification in a destructive agitation, which from a Catholic standpoint seems not only unwarrantable, but more worthy of censure than sympathy. The little Catholicity he had, was unfortunately superficial and feeble and proved unavailing in coping with his impulsive obstinacy. Apostasy seemed the inevitable doom of the arrogant Trustee at that time, nor was Carney to be an exemption. In 1825 his name no longer appears on the list of pew holders,—he drifted further and further from the moorings of his childhood's faith until he wound up his career by refusing priestly ministrations in his dying moments. He died in 1859, and lies buried in the Old (Protestant) Cemetery.

Under the new Trustees, with restored confidence established, the work of completing the Church was pushed forward as vigorously as the untoward circumstances and limited financial resources would permit. The contract for the annex was awarded on St. Patrick's Day, 1823,— but it was not until July, 1825 that it was completed. The Trustees, to keep the public informed of its transactions, especially since it had been so generously helpful in contributing to the improvements, had the event announced in the paper* in this characteristic fashion:

"TO THE PUBLIC.

"With feelings of gratitude and satisfaction we announce to the public that the addition of sixty feet by thirty, to the *Catholic Church of this borough*, which was commenced a considerable time back, is now finished, and that the Church, hitherto entirely too small, is now *sufficiently spacious*, and calculated to admit of Divine Worship being performed in it, with decency and solemnity, which the occasion requires. This we consider our duty to make known to the public in general and to the inhabitants of this borough and its vicinity, in particular; as it is to their generous contributions it is generally indebted for its present prosperous state. Its representatives think the best way to express their gratitude to all its benefactors is, to

---

* *Amer. Volunteer*, July 14, 1825.

inform them that its doors shall be open to all denominations of Christians who may think proper, at any time, to visit it, and conduct themselves while there as Christians.

"N. B.—*The Pews will be rented* on the 7th of August next, when all those (with no exception of persons) who wish to secure to themselves a right to a seat, will please attend at the church."

Carlisle, 11th July, 1825.

[*Signed*.] "TRUSTEES."

As mentioned above, the church was dedicated in August by Bishop Conwell, assisted by Rev. B. Keenan, Lancaster, Rev. Father Dwen, and probably some of the Conewago Fathers.

CHAPTER XIII.

CARLISLE IN THE STRUGGLE FOR CATHOLIC EMANCIPATION.—ORGANIZATION OF THE "CATHOLIC ASSOCIATION OF IRELAND."—PROTESTANTS GENEROUS AND ENTHUSIASTIC IN THE CAUSE.—DANIEL O'CONNELL PROPOSES THEM AS MEMBERS OF THE ASSOCIATION.—THE CORRESPONDENCE GIVEN.

When Daniel O'Connell inaugurated his memorable fight for Catholic Emancipation in 1800,—he had such an instinctive aversion to the violent revolutionary spirit of that period, that his well-known saying, " he would accept of no social amelioration at the cost of a single drop of blood," was looked upon as the mere utterance of a political visionary. Yet from 1822 to 1829 there was a fierce though bloodless battle waged in " old Ireland," one which tried the hearts of Irishmen as much as those who fought at Limerick or Fontenoy. The struggle was gallant, the victory brilliant. Years of harrowing care and persistent disappointment convinced O'Connell that the battle must be a bloodless one, one in which the justice of the cause must be brought strongly and convincingly before the heart of humanity,—one that must enlist the sympathy and aid of every lover of justice and liberty. In 1828 the agitation for Catholic Emancipation reached the culminating point under the persistent and well-directed labors of the Catholic Association, called into life by O'Connell, with ramifications throughout the civilized Christian world. Ireland itself during this time was in a state of seething ferment. It was in June of 1828 that O'Connell, elected by an overwhelming majority to Parliament from County Clare, refused to take the Test oath, which was framed to exclude Catholics from office. Under his magnificent and inspiring generalship Catholic Emancipation was wrung from the reluctant Government. In his gigantic labors the Agitator was finally so successful that the Conservatives, led by such men as Sir Robert Peel and the Duke of Wellington, conceded emancipation on February 6, 1829.

The eyes of the world centered on Ireland during this epoch-making struggle. The heart of every Irishman went out to his far-off home from whence persecution and poverty had exiled him, and now that the fruits of liberty were within sight, within grasp,—he would contribute his share in hastening the blessed hour.

Carlisle, as usual, was one of the first inland towns to take the initiative in joining the Catholic Association,— the potent factor that became an engine of so much happiness to Ireland. It did not wait to take its cue from larger cities, but, fired with the patriotism of its Irish citizens, it modestly but none the less generously sent its contribution to Ireland, and had the supreme satisfaction of not only receiving personal testimonials of appreciation from the great Agitator, by himself proposing them as members of the Catholic Association, but of seeing Emancipation granted. In this effort it will be noticed that creed or church affiliation are set aside, that the Catholic priest and Protestant lawyer meet on the same platform of equality, and that all of them contribute cheerfully to a cause so dear to their hearts,—and one so characteristic of their nationality.

But we will let the newspaper files tell the interesting and touching story:

In the *American Volunteer** we find the subjoined notice in the advertising column:

---

* February 27, 1828.

"CATHOLIC EMANCIPATION.

"The citizens of Carlisle and its vicinity who may be desirous of promoting the object of 'The New Catholic Association of Ireland,' which is composed of Christians of every denomination, are requested to meet at the house of James Bell, Esq., to-morrow (Friday) evening at 6 o'clock."

"MEETING IN CARLISLE, PA.,

"Of the friends of the 'New Catholic Association of Ireland,' February 8, 1828.

"In pursuance of public notice a number of persons, friendly to the new Catholic Association of Ireland, assembled on Friday evening, the 8th instant, at the hotel of Mr. James Bell, in the borough of Carlisle.

"On motion, Mr. James Divin (a Protestant) was called to the chair, and Rev. Patrick J. Dwen appointed secretary.

"The meeting being thus organized, on motion of Mr. John Taylor the following circular was read by the secretary:

"'SIR: Knowing you to be deeply interested in everything connected with the prosperity of Ireland, we take the liberty of soliciting your countenance to the 'New Catholic Association of Ireland,' a sketch of whose object will be seen below.'"

[*Signed.*] "P. KEOGH, *Chairman.*
"JAMES GOWEN, *Secretary.*"

"PHILADELPHIA, January 4th, 1828.

"*Primary* objects of the New Catholic Association of Ireland, which is composed of CHRISTIANS OF ALL DENOMINATIONS,

" 1. To diffuse a liberal and enlightened system of education throughout Ireland.

" 2. To extend Irish commerce.

" 3. To promote Irish agriculture.

" 4. To encourage the consumption of Irish manufactures.

" 5. To encourage, as much as possible, a free and enlightened press, to circulate works calculated to promote just principles, mutual toleration and kindness.

" 6. To preserve the purity of elections in Ireland, especially by supporting the *forty-shilling freeholders* in the maintenance of their just rights.

" 7. To devise means of erecting in Ireland suitable churches for the celebration of Divine Worship and to procure and establish burial grounds wherein the dead may be interred without being liable to any species of insult or contumely.

"8. To ascertain the number of the population of Ireland, the proportion of Catholics and Protestants, and the number of children of each in a course of education.

"Its principal aim is *Universal Emancipation*.

"☞ To constitute membership, *one pound*, Irish currency (according to the present rate of exchange about $5) must be paid on admission.

"Any sum, however small, may nevertheless be contributed towards the funds of the association.

"The following gentlemen are appointed Treasurers, to whom the collecting committees are to pay over the moneys collected, and who are to send the same and the contributors' names to Ireland: General Robert Patterson, General William Duncan, Silas E. Wier, William J. Duane, Joseph M. Doran.

"Mr. Taylor then rose and offered the following preamble and resolutions:

"Whereas, This meeting looks with great confidence to the 'New Catholic Association of Ireland,' and believes its object to be truly philanthropic and humane, and if liberally assisted, as it should be by every lover of freedom, and every comforter of the afflicted, would redound much to the tranquillity and happiness of that oppressed country ; but perfectly aware how unavailing will be its efforts without sufficient funds to enable it to carry its patriotic views into effect ; and knowing it to be, in the present state of affairs, totally inadequate to the accomplishment of its multifarious objects, therefore,

"1. *Resolved*, That to encourage said association to persevere in its great and laudable undertakings, a committee of eight persons, two for each ward in the borough, be appointed to collect the names, places of residence and subscriptions of those gentlemen in Carlisle and its vicinity who may be desirous of becoming members of the association.

"2. *Resolved*, That a treasurer be appointed into whose hands shall be paid all the money which the collecting committee may receive, and whose duty it shall be to send the same, as soon as possible, together with the names, places of birth, and places of residence of the subscribers, to the treasurer of the Association in Philadelphia, requesting them to forward the whole, together with the proceedings of this meeting, to the Treasurer of the Association in Ireland, by the first convenient opportunity.

"3. *Resolved*, That these proceedings be signed by the chairman and secretary, and be published in all the Carlisle papers.

"The above preamble and resolutions were seconded and adopted, and the following gentlemen appointed to act as collecting committee :

"James Givin and Isaac B. Parker, Esq. (Protestants), for the N. W. ward; Colonel Redmond Conyngham and John Taylor (Protestants), for the N. E. ward ; Dr. George D. Foulke and James Underwood, for the S. W. ward ; Cormick McManus (Catholic) and James Bredin (Protestant), for the S. E. ward.

"Isaac B. Parker, Esq., was appointed treasurer.

"It was also agreed that the collecting committee have power to call a meeting of the subscribers whenever they may deem expedient.

"On motion of General Robert McCoy, a subscription paper was opened, and several gentlemen became members of the association on the spot by complying with the conditions, as stated in the above circular.

[*Signed.*] "JAMES GIVIN, *Chairman.*
" PATRICK J. DWEN, *Secretary.*"

The ward committees set to work with a determination to make an active and thorough canvass, and though certain features dwelt upon by the association did not find favor in the eyes of some, still the appeal was so manly, the men interested so zealous, and the object so instinctively dear to the American heart, that the result was a flattering one. Contributions under five dollars were not acknowledged, and from this we can conclude that a generous response on the part of the poorer classes added materially to the success of the enterprise. It is safe to state that probably not one Catholic was unrepresented in that collection. But we again will let the newspaper files* narrate the details:

"THE CAUSE OF IRELAND.

"AUGHINBACH'S INN, CARLISLE, PENN.

"Sept. 13th, 1828.

"In pursuance of a notice a number of those who contributed to the fund of the 'New Catholic Association,' met this evening. James Givin, esq., was called to the chair and Revd. P. J. Dwen appointed secretary.

"Isaac B. Parker, esq., Treasurer of the funds collected in this place submitted the following statement, which was unanimously adopted, and ordered to be published, together with the contributors' names.

"Isaac B. Parker, in account with the contributors to the 'New Catholic Association of Ireland' in Carlisle.

"To cash received from subscribers from the 9th of February till the 14th of March, 1828 . $100.00
" Balance due Treasurer . . .25
$100.25

---

* *American Volunteer*, November 6, 1828.

"March 17th 1828. By cash remitted to Joseph M. Doran, esq., as per receipt . . . $100.00
"By cash for postage 25

"E.E. I. B. Parker $100.25
        "Sept. 18th, 1828.

"Read and approved 13th September, 1828.
[*Signed.*]   "JAMES GIVIN, *Chairman.*"
"Test. P. J. DWEN, *Secy.*"

"Names of contributors copied from Dublin *Weekly Register*" now in our possession : Rev. P. J. Dwen, Gen. Rober McCoy, Isaac B. Parker, esq., James Givin, George D. Foulke, M.D., Cormick McManus, Crawford Foster, Jacob Faust, George Smith, Jr., Gad Day, Samuel McCosky esq., David S. Forney, Robert Snodgrass, John Gillen, John Clark, John Taylor, Redmond Conyngham, James Kernan, (Franklin County), Richard Dougherty, Hugh Gaullaugher, esq., George A. Lyon, esq., James Bredin, Benjamin Stiles, Jacob Bishop, John Irwin, William Irvine, esq., Jacob Hendel, esq., Seawright Ramsey, esq., George Metzger, esq., Thomas Hennessy, John Philips, esq., Geo. Leas, Andrew Carothers.

"The following correspondence, in possession of Mr. John Taylor, was read by him, and ordered by the meeting to be published as a part of its proceedings, *viz* :

"CARLISLE, March 14th, 1828.

"DR. SIR: In conformity with instructions received from Mr. Joseph M. Doran, of your city, I have the pleasure to forward you herewith a draft for One Hundred Dollars, payable to your order, contributed by the " friends of the New Catholic Association of Ireland " residing in Carlisle, Pennsylvania, with a request that their mite be added to the funds of that benevolent and praiseworthy association. You will have the goodness to acknowledge the enclosed, and to inform me whether a more particular designation than that herein noted, will be hereafter necessary to be transmitted to you. I have some small hopes that a farther subscription may be obtained.

"Your obedient & humble servant,
[*Signed.*] "I. B. PARKER."
" TURNER CAMAC, ESQ."

." PHILADELPHIA, March 17th, 1828.

"DEAR SIR: I am requested by Mr. Carmac to acknowledge his receipt of your letter of the 14th inst. enclosing a draft for $100, being the amount contributed by the friends of the New Catholic Association of Ireland, residing in Carlisle and vicinity towards the funds of that society. He begs me to return to the citizens of your borough, through your medium, the thanks of the friends of Ireland of this city, for the ardent and *substantial* manner in which the former have thus generously expressed their devotion to the interests of that unhappy country, and to assure them that the money will be immediately transmitted to Ireland. The description of the contributors is sufficiently precise.

"Respectfully yours,
[*Signed.*] "JOSEPH M. DORAN."
"ISAAC B. PARKER, ESQ."

First remittance to Ireland. Copy of a letter sent to Daniel O'Connell, Esq.

"PHILADELPHIA, June 23rd, 1828.

"DEAR SIR : On behalf, and by direction of the persons whose names, birthplaces and residences, are mentioned below, we have the honor of transmitting to you, for the 'New Catholic Association of Ireland,' for all purposes prohibited by law, a Bill of Exchange for 182£. 8s. 8d. upon London, payable to your order sixty days after sight, dated June 23, 1828 etc., being the net amount of their contributions towards its funds, after deducting expense, etc.

"The contributors, deeply interested as they are in everything connected with the welfare of Ireland, are convinced, after an attentive observation of the progress of affairs in that country for some time past, that the New Catholic Association is eminently calculated to promote its prosperity and richly merits the countenance and support, not only of every Irishman, but also of every individual throughout the world, who desires the melioration of a condition of a very large portion of his fellow-creatures. Under this conviction, sir, and without intending in any wise to interfere with the politics of Ireland, further than these, the expression of their feelings and opinions, they have made their contributions; and there are thousands of others in the United States, who are so disposed and *will shortly* do the same. One feature—an admirable feature—in the Catholic Association, has not escaped the eye of the people of this country, and indeed, has induced many who are not of the Roman Catholic persuasion to become its contributors 'that it is composed of persons of every religious denomination, and it is not deiigned to give benefits and advantages to one sect at the expense of the rest; but is substantially, and in fact, in its object and in its views, Catholic,—in the true sense of the word.' Be assured, the society will have nothing to fear from its enemies, as long as the liberal work shall be impressed upon its front.

"Perhaps it may be proper to remark, that these contributions are by no means to be regarded as emanating from a body or society, they proceed from persons acting entirely *as individuals*, without the consent or connection with each other; and ihould it not be contrary to the rules of the association, it would be gratifying to them to be admitted members for one year, provided that no further payment should be required of them.

"Permit us now in the name of the Irish and their

descendants in the state of Pennsylvania, and for ourselves to heartily thank you, and through you Shiel, and your illustrious friends, for the noble stand you and they have taken for the cause of persecuted Ireland.

"We remain with great respect, sir, your most obedient and humble servants.

[*Signed.*]   "TURNER CARMAC.
                             JOSEPH M. DORAN."
"DANIEL O'CONNELL, ESQ , Dublin."

On the 19th of July, 1828, upwards of one hundred and fifteen gentlemen of Philadelphia and Carlisle (whose names, birthplaces and residences were subsequently inserted in the Dublin papers) were on motion of Daniel O'Connell, Esq., seconded by Sir Francis McDonnell, admitted members of the "Catholic Association of Ireland."

The following resolution was then unanimously adopted, *viz.:*

"*Resolved*, That the thanks of the meeting be tendered to Isaac B. Parker, Esq., for his faithful and punctual attention to the business intrusted to his care at our former meeting.

[*Signed.*]   "JAMES GIVIN, *Chairman.*"
" P. J. DWEN, *Sec'y.*"

FACSIMILE OF MEMBERSHIP CARD OF CATHOLIC ASSOCIATION OF IRELAND.

www.ingramcontent.com/pod-product-compliance
Lightning Source LLC
Chambersburg PA
CBHW020822230426
43666CB00007B/1054